South Beach Recipes

Not Low Fat, Not No Carb...

Recipes for a food plan you can live with
...... forever!

Nancy McC

Aglob Publishing

Aglob Publishing
Hallandale Beach, Florida
Tel: 954-456-1476
E-Mail: info@aglobpublishing.com
www.aglobpublishing.com

Library of Congress Cataloging-in-Publication Data

McCune, Nancy.
  South beach recipes, not low fat, not no carb : recipes for a food
plan you can live with--forever! / Nancy McCune.
     p. cm.
  ISBN 1-59427-014-7
1. Reducing diets--Recipes. 2. Weight loss. I. Title.

RM222.2.M43385 2003
641.5'635--dc22

                                                    2003021502

Manufactured in the United States of America
5 4 3 2 1

Acknowledgements

To John, Your love, your support, your inspiration, allow me to live my dreams.

To Irene, Thanks for being my friend, no matter what.

To my Clients, Thanks for letting me try out these recipes and thanks for proving that this plan really does work... for everyone.

About The Author

From childhood Nancy knew she had a gift that made her different from other people. Her intuitive ability to help and heal people has always come natural to her. After 20 successful years in Corporate America, she felt that something was missing in her life. To find what was missing, she began to explore the various healing modalities that would work alongside her natural gift to heal. This path has led her to an intense and comprehensive study of the healing arts and sciences. Nancy began to blend her gifts with her newfound knowledge, achieving her goal to assist others to attain health, wellness and a new sense of empowerment over their lives. Nancy has a love of books, meeting new people and learning about them. She enjoys golf, tennis, scuba diving, and sharing her life with the love of her life, John. Having no tolerance for the cold, she has found her paradise in South Florida. Nancy is a gourmet cook and having friends in for dinner parties is a passion for her. She takes time every day to appreciate all the good things in her life and having the ability to recognize them!

Contents

Breakfast

Lunch And Dinner

Veggies

Salads

Snacks

Why I wrote this book...

Let me tell you a story. This is about a person who has fought the weight battle for most of her life. This is my story. Even in my teen years in the early 60's I struggled. Back then we did diet pills and after a stint on them you slept for a week and ate everything you could get in your mouth.

In the late 60's I married, had a child and the weight really began to climb. Back to diet pills. They made me so hyper that one day I found myself out in the yard scrubbing the chain link fence with a toothbrush. That's when I made the decision that they just weren't for me.

Then I did the divorce diet. But of course when I got over the marriage, I got over the diet and the weight crept back on. Now it's the early 80's and I found hypnosis.

Hypnosis Works!! And it's a good thing too, as I was now at the 266 mark! I used hypnosis to successfully shed 116# in a little less than a year. I never told anyone that I used hypnosis because back then it was way to airy-fairy and now I was in corporate America with all the added stress of being a single parent. The only way to keep my weight to a manageable level was to starve myself. And I did.

Ten years later I remarried and had a new husband and a stepson to feed on top of my daughter, and so starving myself went out the window and this time I found exercise. Running... shin splints, blisters, but using hypnosis and running made it work at least for a while... As the 80's drew to a close exercise became less and less effective.

13

I developed my ability to cook to the gourmet level and could put together a party for 150 in the blink of an eye. Had to taste everything along the way, didn't I? And after all, aren't most gourmet chefs a little on the heavy side? Gave me a great excuse to be fat!

Then in 88 came the second divorce diet. Now this one I could really do because I was very familiar with the starvation routine! My daughter had gone to college by now and I had taken a step up the corporate ladder and with that, in 89, came a move to Miami.

About this time I found working out with weights and the low fat/high carb diet. Now I was really in trouble. I wasn't taking in enough protein to build muscle and so some other metabolic things began to happen.

…Went on the latest diet drug craze and it didn't work for me. Thankfully, I didn't stay on it long enough to suffer any damage to my body. I was reasonably thin as I started my relationship with John but as we became partners in life other things filled my exercise time.

I turned 50. Now the weight crept up no matter how little I ate. Waistline and midriff expanding, can't get my britches buttoned and hungry 24/7. I just couldn't imagine why. I watched the fats, ate lots of carbs and had no energy. None.

In 97 came a big career move. I became a refugee from Corporate America and studied to become a hypnotist. I opened my practice but began to shy away from weight reduction clients, as I didn't seem to be making a difference for them. I couldn't recommend a "diet" that worked! And as I got heavier and heavier I could hardly set an example for anyone else, so I stopped doing weight reduction clients. I had now increased my power walking

14

to 35 miles during the average week and those little walking shorts got tighter and tighter!

I continued to create CD's related to weight reduction and people responded vary favorably to them but I still didn't have the answer with a food plan. Some part of me knew that no matter how good a hypnotist I was, until I could tie it up with a food plan I would never have the ultimate answer.

I began to read everything on weight reduction. Every popular book, every medical research paper. Most plans were boring, some were expensive, all presumed that after a time you would go off them, back to "regular" eating and I knew that the weight would come piling back on. No, I needed a plan to live with forever... I needed to find something permanent.

I began to realize that I didn't need a No Fat/High Carb plan or a High Fat/No Carb Plan. I needed to learn about healthy fat and healthy carbs and I needed a way to stop being hungry all the time.

I studied all the popular low carb plans and found I could use my talent as a gourmet cook to make food interesting and taste good, too. And it worked... in three weeks I was back into a size 10. And the best part for me was that I have more energy than I can ever remember having. Good energy, not hyped pill energy.

As an experienced dieter, way too experienced, I know that there are three things that will derail a diet:

- Deprivation
- Lack of results
- Boredom

Lets look at deprivation… If you feel deprived, even for one second, the subconscious mind will drive you to the nearest cookie. Believe it. Your subconscious mind has only one primary goal… keeping you happy and satisfied. A state known as homeostasis. Balance. So when others are having dessert and you're not, the subconscious is setting up to derail your efforts.

The subconscious is ultimately in control in every situation. You'll be putting that cookie in your mouth and chewing it before your conscious mind knows what is happening.

I can hear you saying, Nancy, what about "will power"? Well, will power is highly overrated!! Let me tell you what will power really is… Will Power is based in the conscious mind and is a short term burst of determination that gets you started on a project. If the subconscious is not in agreement with the conscious, the project will soon fail.

This is where hypnosis and the CD's I have created come in. (www.nancymccune.com/WeightLoss) They allow the subconscious to give up the idea that fat is OK and get into agreement with the conscious that thin is good.

Let's look at lack of results… If the weight creeps downward at a pace of a few ounces a week especially in the beginning, the subconscious is very likely to say. "Told ya so. Nothing works for you. You are so hungry. Have another cookie, you'll feel better."

Low carb eating gives great, ego strengthening results, from the first day. When you see your belly shrinking and the scale dropping 8-12#'s in the first two weeks with no hunger and loads of energy, you are motivated to continue. At about the end of the second week you can really mentally begin to savor your ultimate success.

Now let's look at boredom… this one will derail you because as humans we just don't like being bored. Don't eat plain food. Yes, you can do this food plan by eating nothing but chicken and broccoli, but why would you want to? By the time you have shed all the weight you want, you will realize that this plan is meant for a life long way of eating. After all, why would you stop? You're happy, healthy, thin, full and satisfied.

I have gone through all my favorite recipes, been given recipes, made up recipes and generally made a compilation of every type of recipe I can find to give you loads of variety so that you will never, ever be bored.

The best advice I can give you now is to give it a try… Get yourself some additional support by using my CDs and finally find that South Beach Body under the fat.

Ultimate success is so close…

Enjoy!

Nancy

Kitchen Equipment
to make your life a lot easier...

A Misto — This little device allows you to spray the oil of your choice just as you would Pam. Now, no disrespect to Pam but wouldn't you rather know you are getting pure, no chemicals, and your choice of wonderful olive oil? You can get one at a kitchen store or I have seen them on ebay.

An Ice Cream Maker — You will not feel deprived when you can have some ice cream in the second and third phase of this plan. Look on ebay.

Omelet Pan – You will be making a lot of these so get yourself a good pan.

Parchment Paper – This makes a good cookie sheet liner for either baking or freezing.

Foil Baking Cups – Yes, you really do need foil. The paper kind stick no matter what you do!

Plastic Sandwich Bags – Great for making individual servings and freezing them.

Food Information

T hroughout these recipes you will see brand names mentioned. This is simply because it was what I could find while testing recipes. I am not endorsing any particular brand or putting down another. I'm just not going to write out Granulated Artificial Sweetener when I can type Splenda! Use whatever you prefer as long as it minimizes the bad fat and bad carbs that you have learned about.

Experiment with spices and seasonings. Buy the freshest, best quality you can afford and try different ones in a dish. DON'T EAT PLAIN FOOD! You'll get bored and that defeats the whole purpose of this book.

Ricotta. You are going to use a lot of this so shop around for the one you like the best. Please don't give up on ricotta if the first one you try is gritty or off flavor. Try another until one suits you.

I buy turkey sausage in the one-pound tube in the freezer case. Cut it in six slices and lay them out on a piece of saran or parchment. Turn on the faucet, wet your hand with cold water and pat them out to the desired thickness. Keep wetting your hand so the meat doesn't stick.

Cook them all at once in a large frying pan and freeze them individually in those little sandwich bags that you bought on the equipment page. Easily reheated in the microwave... Much cheaper than the store bought brown-n-serve.

Buy turkey bacon and cook all of it in the oven on a cookie sheet lined with parchment. Package it in plastic bags for speed and convenience. Keep it in the freezer.

19

Eggs or Not! Eggbeaters and other cholesterol free egg products are really wonderful. Less calories, less fat but for me at least, less appealing so sometimes I use ½ the quantity for a 2-egg omelet and then use a real egg. Not every time though... remember what I told you about deprivation.

Nuts to you!! Try out some of the recipes using bulk Almonds from the grocery. Package 15 in a snack size bag. Bag up the whole recipe and then you have a take along snack. Don't allow yourself to be hungry, but don't put your hand into a bowl full of nuts and think you'll stop at 15. Do the same with pistachios but put thirty in the bag.

Tomato Products... All canned and jarred tomato products contain some sugar, which is natural in the tomato. Buy the ones that are "no sugar" added or make your own.

A question from many clients, "Why can't I get Jell-O without the Nutrasweet?" Many are allergic to aspartame and would so love to have Jell-O without it. Here is the solution: Buy a box of Knox PLAIN gelatin packets. Use just like Jell-o by mixing in unsweetened Kool-Aid and either Stevia or Splenda to taste. It works perfectly!

Save the whites of the eggs when you make the ice cream recipes. Perfect in your omelets. You can freeze egg whites for use later!

Tahini. This is an ingredient in humus and is simply a paste made from sesame seeds. Find it in the exotic foods isle or look in the health food isle many grocery stores have now.

Coleslaw. If you like coleslaw make your own. Do not under any circumstances eat this in a restaurant. It has sugar... lots!

Sambal Olek. Get to know this interesting stuff. Available in an oriental grocery store or sometimes in the exotic foods section of your regular grocery, this is a wonderful chili garlic paste that livens up anything you put it in.

Meatballs. So convenient, packed frozen in bags... you need to skip these until later in the program. They contain wheat flour and too many carbs for the first phase.

Ground meat, hamburger. Be aware of the fat content of these products. The lower the price, the more fat. Here it is in escalating fat content: Ground Round, Ground Sirloin, Ground Chuck, and Ground Meat.

Breakfast Recipes

<u>Vegetable Quiche</u> *(Individual Servings)*

Although this recipe appears in other books, I include it as I have adapted the preparation method to one I feel is a little easier

1 package (10 ounces) frozen chopped spinach
3/4 cup liquid egg substitute
3/4 cup shredded reduced-fat cheese
1/4 cup diced green bell peppers
1/4 cup diced onion

Preheat oven 350 degrees.

Microwave the spinach for 2 1/2 minutes on high. Drain excess liquid. Squeeze dry.

Line a 12-section muffin pan with <u>foil</u> cups. Spray the cups with cooking spray.

Divide cheese, peppers, onions, and spinach among the cups. Don't worry about mixing the ingredients before you fill the cups. Pour egg over vegetable mixture. Bake at 350 degrees for 20 minutes, until a knife inserted comes out clean.

Quiche cups can be frozen and reheated in the microwave (remove the foil first).

Any combination of appropriate vegetables and reduced-fat cheeses may be used.

Add some lean ham, turkey bacon that is precooked, turkey cold cuts etc.

Here is a variation: Prepare to just before baking and freeze instead but use paper-baking cups. Take out what you need and put them directly into your microwave for 2 minutes. Some people like the texture even better this way.

Mock Danish

1 egg,
1 Tbsp Splenda,
1 tsp vanilla,
a drop of lemon juice,
2 ounces of reduced fat cream cheese, divided use
A sprinkle of cinnamon

Place one ounce of the cream cheese in a microwavable bowl and melt carefully on low. Mix until smooth and being sure the mixture is just barely warm mix in the egg, Splenda, vanilla, and lemon juice. Sprinkle with cinnamon.

Then chop the second ounce of cream cheese and stir in gently –You could use cottage cheese just fine for this -- then if you want, drop in a few small globs of sugar free jelly (only if you are in phase two).

Pour in a Pam-sprayed bowl and microwave 2 minutes.

This does not have an "eggy" consistency.

Greek "Spanakopita" Veggie Quiches

12 eggs, beaten
A bag of pre-washed Spinach, sautéed in olive oil and drained
1 med. chopped onion, sauté this along with the spinach
fat-free feta cheese (I used the kind with sun-dried tomatoes and black olives in it)
juice from one lemon
a little olive oil
½ cup light cream
butter-flavor spray
oregano (fresh is really good, but dried is just fine)
black pepper

Mix this all together and bake just like the veggie quiches.

It comes out very much resembling one of my favorite Greek foods "Spanakopita", just without the phyllo dough.

You can adjust the quantity of spinach and feta, using the eggs mainly to bind the little quiches together or but you could make it eggier if you like.

Do NOT skimp on lemon juice, oregano, and pepper. These seasonings are what give it that really Greek flavor.

Tzaziki Sauce as is traditionally served in Greek restaurants.
Mix plain yogurt,
a little olive oil,
chopped cucumbers,

onion,
and black pepper.

Be careful with the Tzaziki until you get to the second
phase.

Yummy Weekend Breakfast

18 ounces sliced smoked chicken breast
12 stalks steamed broccoli
6 tomato slices
6 poached eggs
1/2 cup roasted bell pepper hollandaise (see below)

On each warmed plate place 3 ounces sliced smoked chicken, sliced tomato, and two stalks of broccoli on each warmed plate (arrange broccoli to provide "walls"). Place poached eggs between broccoli stalks (or "walls"). Pour 2 Tbsp of hollandaise over eggs. Garnish with a sprig of basil or edible flower.

6 Servings

Roasted Bell Pepper Hollandaise

6 egg yolks
  2 Tbsp lemon juice
  1 cup I can't believe its not Butter
  1 large roasted bell pepper
  1/2 to 1 cup coarsely chopped fresh basil
  Dash red pepper

Roast bell pepper (peel, seed,). Place pepper and basil in blender and blend until pureed with yolks and lemon juice. Melt butter until really hot. Start blender on low setting and slowly pour the melted butter through the top. Start with just a few drops and as it thickens you can increase speed of blender and pour the butter in a small stream.

Serve immediately.

Eggs Benedict
Serves 4

1 tsp. Vinegar

8 Eggs

1 cup fresh Spinach Leaves washed, stems removed

8 slices Farmer John® Canadian Bacon

8 slices Low Fat Havarti or Low Fat Muenster Cheese

In a large skillet over medium high heat, bring 2 inches of water and the vinegar to a boil.

Reduce water to a simmer; add eggs one by one to the simmering water.

Cook eggs for 4-5 minutes. The whites should be firm and the yolks should be slightly runny.

In a non-stick skillet, heat Canadian bacon until warm.

To assemble the Eggs Benedict place two slices Canadian bacon on a plate; add a few spinach leaves and two poached eggs.

Pour 1 Tbsp warm sauce over and garnish with paprika and fresh parsley.

Hollandaise Sauce

3 Egg Yolks
  1 Tbsp. hot Water
  1 Tbsp. fresh Lime Juice
  Dash of Hot Sauce
  Salt and freshly ground Black
    Pepper to Taste
1/4 tsp. Paprika
1/4 cup fresh chopped

For the sauce: Place the yolks, water and lemon juice in a blender or food processor.

Blend on medium speed for one minute.

With the blender running, pour the hot, melted butter through the opening in the lid of the blender.

Season with hot sauce, salt and pepper. Keep warm

Wild Mushroom Frittata

1 ¼ cups egg substitute
¼ tsp. Salt
¼ tsp. Pepper
1 tbsp. Olive oil
3/4 lbs. Assorted mushrooms (portabella, shiitake, cremini, etc.) Coarsely chopped
1 shallot thinly sliced
1/2 tsp oregano
1/4 cup shredded low fat mozzarella cheese
1 tbsp. Grated parmesan cheese
1 tbsp. Chopped fresh basil

Preheat the broiler.
Heat the oil in a medium nonstick skillet with an ovenproof handle.

Add the mushrooms, shallot, and oregano.

Sauté until mushrooms are golden, about five minutes.

Add the egg to the mushrooms.

Reduce heat and cook without stirring until the eggs are set, 2-5 minutes.

Sprinkle with the mozzarella, Parmesan and basil. Broil the frittata 5 inches from the heat, until top is lightly browned, and puffed about 2 minutes.

Allow to stand 5 minutes before serving.

Makes 2 servings

Pumpkin Quiche Morning Treats

This is only for phase three because of the glycemic index of pumpkin. (107)

1 15oz can 100% Pure Pumpkin
1 cup liquid egg substitute (= to 4 eggs)
½ tsp cinnamon
¼ tsp ginger
tiny pinch cloves
(or use "pumpkin pie spice")
½ tsp salt

Preheat oven 350 degrees.

Blend ingredients together with a whisk.

Line a 12-section muffin pan with **foil** cups.

Spray the cups with cooking spray.

Divide mixture evenly among the muffin cups.

Bake at 350 degrees for 20 minutes, until a knife inserted comes out clean.

Refrigerate.

Lunch and Dinner

Baked Salmon

2 cloves garlic minced
6 tbsp olive oil
1 tsp dried basil
1 tsp salt
1 tsp ground black pepper
1 tbsp lemon juice
1 tbsp fresh parsley (chopped).
2 (6 ounce) salmon fillets

In a medium glass bowl, prepare marinade by mixing garlic, olive oil, basil, salt, pepper, lemon juice and parsley.

Place salmon filets in medium size plastic bag, and cover with marinade.

Marinate in the fridge about 1 hour turning occasionally.

Preheat oven to 375

Place fillets in aluminum foil.

Cover with marinade and seal.

Place sealed salmon in the glass dish and bake 25-35 min until easily flaked with a fork.

Simple Sautéed Chicken Breast

Balsamic vinegar
olive oil
some rosemary
Montreal steak seasoning.

Mix together in a plastic bag
Add thinly sliced chicken breast and marinate about 15-20
minutes.

Then sauté it in a frying pan.

Onion-Rubbed Flank Steak

1/3 cup chopped onion
1 tbsp red wine vinegar or cider vinegar
1 tbsp canola oil
1 tsp pepper
1/2 tsp salt
1 garlic clove, minced
¼ tsp dried rosemary, crushed
¼ tsp dried basil
1 beef flank steak (1-1/2 pounds)

In the bowl of your food processor, combine the first eight ingredients; process until nearly smooth, brush over both sides of steak.

Place in a large re-sealable plastic bag; seal bag and refrigerate for 3-4 hours or overnight.

Place steak on a broiler pan. Broil 3-4 in. from the heat for 6-8 minutes on each side or until meat reaches desired doneness (for rare, a meat thermometer should read 140°; medium, 160°; well-done, 170°).

Thinly slice across the grain.

Yield: 6 servings.

Montego Bay Chicken

¼ cup reduced-sodium soy sauce
¼ cup lime juice
2 tbsp Splenda
2 garlic cloves, minced
1 tsp hot pepper sauce
1 tsp rum extract
¼ tsp ground ginger or 1 tsp minced fresh gingerroot
4 boneless skinless chicken breast halves (4 ounces each)

In a large re-sealable plastic bag, combine the first seven ingredients; add the chicken.

Seal bag and turn to coat; refrigerate for at least 2 hours.

Drain and discard marinade.

Coat grill rack with nonstick cooking spray before starting the grill.

Grill chicken, uncovered, over indirect medium heat for 6-8 minutes on each side or until juices run clear.

Yield: 4 servings.

Mexican Meatloaf

1 lb. lean ground sirloin
1 can (14.5 oz) diced tomatoes (drained)
1/3 cup of diced onions
1 envelope (1.25 oz) Old El Paso Taco Seasoning Mix
(reduced sodium)
1 egg (slightly beaten)
1/3 cup low-fat cheddar cheese (shredded)

Preheat oven to 350 degrees.

Combine sirloin, tomatoes, onions, taco seasoning and egg
in a bowl.

Mix ingredients thoroughly.

Press mixture into an un-greased 9x5x3-baking pan.

Bake for 50 minutes at 350 degrees.

Remove from oven and sprinkle cheese on top.

Serve with salsa or low-fat sour cream and steamed
veggies of your choice.

London Broil

1 Flank Steak any size, sliced into very thin slices, if you partially freeze it this will be a lot easier!

1 lb of turkey bacon cut into thirds.

Brush a little mustard on each slice of meat and add a slice of turkey bacon, roll up and secure with a toothpick.

When all slices are rolled up, brown them in a large skillet

Put into a crock-pot with 1/2 cup of water; add garlic powder and some Adobo seasoning and let cook all day!!

The meat comes out VERY tender and yummy!!!!

This can be served to the family with Rice or Noodles and you can enjoy yours with a veggie on the side.

Crab Stuffed Mushrooms

12-14 medium size mushrooms
4.25 oz. can of crab meat (drained)
2 garlic gloves (finely diced)
3 green onions (finely diced)
1 tbsp. olive oil
1 tbsp. mayonnaise
1 tsp. lemon juice
3 tbsp. Parmesan cheese
1/2 tsp. cayenne pepper
butter ("I Can't Believe It's Not Butter")

Wash and pat dry mushrooms.

Remove stems.

Finely dice half (6-7) of the mushroom stems.

Sauté mushroom stems, garlic and green onions in olive oil.

In a medium bowl combine crab, mayonnaise, lemon juice, Parmesan cheese and cayenne pepper.

Add the mushroom stems, garlic and green onions.

Stir together all ingredients.

Lightly brush the bottom only of a shallow, glass-baking dish with butter.

Lightly brush the cavity side of each mushroom with butter.

Generously fill each mushroom with mixture using a small melon scoop and place in glass baking dish.

Bake at 375 degrees for 15 min.

Halupki

1 pound of lean ground beef or turkey, browned well and drained of all fat.
½ small head of cabbage cut into 1-2" pieces.
1 small can sauerkraut (drain and rinse with water to take out some of the salt)
one large can of diced tomatoes.

Layer in order, 1/3 cabbage, kraut, meat and tomatoes until you get 3 layers and then end with tomatoes. You can season as you go with salt, pepper, garlic or whatever you wish. Cover with foil very tightly and bake in a 350-degree oven for 3-4 hours.

In the second and third phase you can add about 1/3 cup of raw brown rice to the layers and this makes it taste more like the traditional "Halupki"

Inside-out Cabbage Rolls

1lb of lean ground round or ground lean turkey
1 sliced onion, until browned.
1 sliced medium cabbage
2 cups of V8. (More or less V8 depending on how "soupy" you want the dish)

Sauté ground meat with onion until browned.

Drain off the fat.

Stir in cabbage.

Season to taste with salt, pepper and herbs (recommended: thyme and a bay leaf, or Italian seasoning and garlic powder...maybe some parsley).

Cover and simmer until cabbage is tender.

Serve as is, or topped with a spoonful of fat free sour cream.

Meatloaf

2 lbs ground sirloin
1/2 green pepper minced fine
1 stalk celery minced fine
1 small onion minced fine
1/2 of a small zucchini grated-skin and all!
2 eggs
enough V-8 to moisten
1 Tbsp. Italian seasoning
4 Tbsp. Parmesan cheese

Mix altogether and form into loaf. Put into a pan and pour a little V-8 over to keep it from drying out. Bake about 1-1/2 hours at 350*.

Grilled Flank Steak

1 pound lean flank steak
3/4 cup red wine
3 garlic cloves, cut into quarters
1 bay leaf, cut in half
1 tsp onion powder
2 tsp Dijon mustard

Marinate steak in baking dish with wine, garlic, and bay leaf for 1 hour.

Preheat broiler.

Drain steak.

Place steak on broiler rack.

Sprinkle with onion powder.

Spread a thin layer of mustard over the top.

Grill to desired doneness.

45

Salsa Chicken

2 pounds chicken breast tenders (or about 6 chicken breasts cut into strips)
1 cup Salsa (see sauce section)
1 can Diet Coke, caffeine free

Spray a pan with PAM and sauté the chicken tenders till they turn white and there is no pink showing, but they're still not fully cooked and the liquid is almost gone;

Add the coke and salsa

Bring to a boil; simmer; cover; cook till the liquid is reduced for approx an hour or so.

Serve hot with some sauce next to green salad or other of your favorite steamed veggies. It's also good cold mixed with the salad greens as a type of taco salad without the chips of course! The sauce becomes the dressing.

The mix of coke and salsa works with any type meat. With ground meat, it's a Sloppy Joe. It's good with beef and pork too. More coke and less salsa create more of a BBQ flavor.

Pork and Black Bean Chili

This is a 2nd or 3rd phase recipe

1 pound lean boneless pork loin roast
16 ounces salsa
2 15 oz cans no-salt-added black beans undrained
1 cup chopped yellow bell peppers
¾ cup chopped onion
1 tsp ground cumin
1 tsp chili powder
1 tsp dried oregano
¼ cup fat free sour cream
Low Fat Shredded Cheddar for garnish

Trim fat from pork; cut pork into 1-inch pieces.

Combine pork and next 7 ingredients in a 4-quart electric slow cooker; stir well.

Cover with lid; cook on low-heat setting for 8 hours or until pork is tender.
Ladle chili into bowls; top with sour cream.

Sprinkle on a little low fat cheddar cheese

Yield: 4 servings (serving size: 2 cups chili and 1 tbsp sour cream)

Chicken Breasts With Cucumber Relish

1 cucumber
1 tbsp. chopped fresh parsley
1 tbsp. chopped red onion
¼ tsp. red pepper flakes
Salt and pepper
1 lb. boneless, skinless chicken breasts
½ tsp. ground cumin
1 tbsp. butter
1 tbsp. olive oil

Peel and chop cucumber very fine.

Combine with onion, parsley, red pepper flakes and ½ tsp salt.

Sprinkle chicken with cumin, ½ tsp salt and ¼ tsp pepper.

Heat butter and oil in frying pan over medium heat.

Sauté chicken until browned, about 5 minutes per side.

Serve with cucumber and onion relish.

Chicken Cacciatore

4 chicken breasts, boned and skinned
2 tbsp. Olive oil
½ cup chicken broth
½ cup water
1 cup sliced mushrooms
1 c. sliced green pepper
1 sliced med. onion
2 c. spaghetti sauce (purchased or homemade, please check store bought for sugar and carb content)

Melt butter in skillet over medium heat.

Add chicken breasts and broth.

Cover and simmer 20 minutes.

In another pan, bring water to a boil.

Add mushrooms, peppers, and onion.

Simmer for 5 minutes.

Drain well and add spaghetti sauce.

Return to heat and stir until thoroughly heated.

To serve, place 3 heaping tbsp of sauce over each chicken breast portion and serve immediately.

Serves 4

Lime Baked Catfish

1 Tbsp Smart Balance margarine
2 Tbsp lime juice
¼ tsp pepper
¼ tsp garlic powder
2 catfish fillets
(I get mine from Sam's or Costco) Boneless and skinless.
Portion controlled so you can take what you want out of
the bag)

Heat oven to 375 degrees

Melt margarine in a saucepan.

Stir in lime juice, pepper and garlic powder; mix well.

Remove from heat and set aside.

Place fillets in a shallow baking dish.

Brush each generously with lime sauce.

Bake for 12-14 minutes or until fish flakes easily

Remove to a warm serving dish; spoon pan juices over
each fillet.

Serves 2

Grilled Swordfish

2 tbsp balsamic vinegar
2 tbsp lemon juice
2 tbsp lime juice
1 tbsp olive oil- plus 1 tsp
4 cloves garlic, minced
¼ tsp white pepper, optional
1 tbsp ginger root, minced OR
1 tsp powdered ginger
lemon wedges for garnish
lime wedge for garnish
4-5 ounce Swordfish, Shark, or Mahi-mahi fillets

In a plastic bag combine vinegar, lemon & lime juices, oil, garlic, ginger root, & pepper.

Add fish. Turn to coat w/ marinade.

Cover & refrigerate at least 20 minutes, turning occasionally.

After 20 minutes, drain & discard any remaining marinade.

Spray grill rack w/ PAM or your Misto.

Place grill rack 5" from coals.

Grill fish 4 minutes on each side, until cooked through.

Transfer to serving platter.

Garnish with lime & lemon wedges.

51

Crock Pot Fajitas

1 ½ lb. boneless sirloin steak, cut into thin strips
2 Tbsp. olive oil
2 Tbsp. lemon juice
2 cloves garlic, minced
1 ½ tsp. seasoned salt
½ tsp. chili powder
¼ tsp. cumin
1 large green pepper, cut into long, narrow strips
1 red pepper, cut into strips
1 jalapeno pepper, chopped
1 large onion, cut into long, narrow strips
6 to 8 (7 inch) whole wheat tortillas for the family and
fresh steamed veggies for you

Garnish:
Reduced Fat Cheddar cheese, shredded
Salsa
Fat Free Sour cream
Lettuce, shredded
Tomatoes, diced

In a skillet over medium heat, brown the steak in oil.

Place steak and drippings in crock-pot. Add lemon juice,
garlic, salt, chili powder, cumin, green pepper & red
pepper, jalapeno pepper and onion.

Cover and cook on high for 3 to 4 hours until meat is very
tender.

Warm tortillas according to package directions;

Let each family member build their own fajita with toppings of cheese, salsa, sour cream, lettuce and tomatoes.

Fold in sides of the tortilla and serve immediately.

You can skip the tortillas and have a nice vegetable with yours.

Southwestern Grouper with Tomatillos and Avocado

Perfect for a dinner party!

1 ¼ to 1 ½ pounds grouper; 4 fillets
Coarse salt
Ground pepper
1 tsp ground cumin,
½ tsp sweet paprika,
2 tbsp extra-virgin olive oil,
1 lime, halved
½ medium red onion, chopped
1 jalapeno or Serrano pepper, seeded, finely chopped
2 or 3 large cloves garlic, finely chopped
8 to 10 tomatillos, husks peeled and diced
½ Michelob Ultra beer
2 tbsp chopped cilantro leaves
a few sprigs for garnish

Filling for Avocado
1 tbsp extra-virgin olive oil
½ red onion, chopped
1 jalapeno, seeded and finely chopped
1 small red bell pepper, seeded and chopped
A sprinkle of Splenda
Dash cayenne pepper
Salt
2 tbsp butter
2 ripe avocados
1 lime, juiced

Season fish with salt, pepper, cumin, and paprika.

Heat a nonstick skillet over medium high heat.

Add 1 tbsp oil.

Heat an ovenproof serving plate in a warm oven.

Sauté fish 3 minutes on each side or until opaque.

Squeeze the juice of 1/2 lime over the fish and carefully slide the fillets onto warm platter.

Cover the fish to keep it warm. Return pan to heat and add remaining tbsp of oil.

Over medium high heat, quickly sauté the red onion, jalapeno and the garlic. Sauté a minute or so and then add the diced tomatillos with seeds and juices. Season mixture with coarse salt and Sauté the mixture of vegetables 5 minutes.

Once you get the sauce cooking, heat a second skillet over moderate heat for your Avocado filling.

Add 1 tbsp extra-virgin olive oil, chopped onion, jalapeno and red bell pepper. Sauté 2 or 3 minutes.

Combine peppers and onions. Season with a sprinkle of Splenda, a dash of cayenne pepper and salt.

When mixture bubbles, reduce heat to simmer. Cut butter into pieces and stir into mixture. Allow mixture to simmer and cook until creamy, 5 to 7 minutes.

While sauce is cooking, go back to your sauce for the fish.

Add the beer and the juice of 1/2 lime and cilantro to the pan.

Simmer sauce 5 minutes longer, and then spoon hot sauce over the fish filets.

Garnish platter with a few extra sprigs of the cilantro.

Cut avocados in 1/2 lengthwise and remove pits. Squeeze limejuice over the avocados to keep them from browning and season them with a little coarse salt. Arrange on the serving plate.

To serve, fill the avocados, allowing the vegetables to spill down and over the sides of the avocado onto the serving platter. The ripe avocado is spooned away from its skin with bites of creamy, warm peppers. Place the avocados alongside garnished fish.

Roasted Chicken

2 chicken breasts, on the bone and with skin
4 paper thin lemon slices
8 cloves garlic, thinly sliced
4 sprigs thyme or any fresh herb you like
Coarse grained salt and cracked black pepper
1 cup fat-free, low sodium chicken broth
1 lemon, juiced
Preheat oven to 450 degrees F.

Slide 2 fingers under chicken skin and loosen enough to tuck 2 lemon slices, 4 garlic slices and 1thyme sprig underneath the skin, directly over the breast meat of each chicken breast.

Season chicken generously with salt and pepper.

Place chicken in 9 by 13- inch glass baking dish.

Pour 1 cup chicken broth, remaining sliced garlic and thyme sprigs in pan bottom.

Place in oven and roast until chicken is golden brown and cooked through, about 25 minutes.

Remove chicken from pan and set aside.

Pour pan juices into a small saucepot.

Add lemon juice.

Reduce over medium high heat until sauce has thickened to almost a glaze.

Taste and adjust seasonings with salt and pepper.

Pour juices over chicken and serve immediately.

Summer Chicken with
Fresh Tomato Mayonnaise

¾ pound boneless, skinless chicken breasts
1-cup fat-free, low-sodium chicken broth
1 medium tomato
¼ cup low fat mayonnaise
Salt and freshly ground black pepper

Place chicken in a small saucepan.

Add the chicken broth. The chicken should be covered with broth If not, add water to cover chicken.

Bring the broth to a gentle simmer and cook chicken 5 minutes. Remove from the beat and let cool in the broth for at least 10 minutes.

Cut the tomato in half, scoop out the seeds and pulp of one half and pulse in a food processor or press through a sieve or food mill.

Cut the remaining tomato half into cubes.

Mix 2/3 cup tomato puree with the mayonnaise until smooth. Add salt and pepper to taste.

Remove chicken from broth, save 2 tbsp broth for the rice and sprinkle chicken with salt and pepper to taste.

Place on 2 dinner plates and spoon sauce over the top. Sprinkle the tomato cubes over the sauce.

Makes 2 servings.

Serve with Rice Salad for 2nd and 3rd Phase or with a nice mixed green salad for first phase.

Baked Red Snapper Spanish Style

Very Garlicky!

6 snapper fillets, 6-10 oz. each
2 medium onions, sliced 1/4" thick
2 green peppers, sliced in 1/4" thick rounds
¾ cup lemon juice mixed with 1 cup water
1 whole head fresh garlic, peeled and or mashed
1 (14-16 oz.) can whole tomatoes in juice, crushed
salt pepper
paprika
¼ Cup Olive Oil

Preheat oven to 3500F.

Arrange fish in pan and season with salt and pepper.

Place onions and peppers on top of fish.

Mix garlic and lemon juice together and pour over fish.

Sprinkle with paprika.

Pour on olive oil.

Bake 20 to 30 minutes or until fish is just done.

Serves: 6

Preparation: 15 minutes
Cooking: 20 to 30 minutes

Sautéed Yellowtail

This is an elegant presentation fit for any dinner party. This is a 3rd phase recipe

2 lbs. yellowtail fillets (or other firm white fish)
Lemon juice
Salt
White pepper
3 Tbsp flour
1 egg beaten with a little milk
butter for sautéing
4 slices of tomato per serving
½ small avocado per serving, cut in 1/4" thick slices
Béarnaise sauce (see sauces)
lemon slices
fresh parsley, chopped

Preheat oven to 450F.

Season the fillets in a mixture of lemon juice, salt and white pepper.

Sprinkle with flour and then shake off and discard excess

Dip in beaten egg.

Heat the butter and Sauté the fish on only one side.

Place sautéed side down in an oiled baking dish and pour the pan juices over the fish.

Top with a layer of tomato slices and then avocado.

Bake 8 to 10 minutes.

When done, remove from the heat and top with béarnaise sauce. (see sauces)

Put under broiler until just browned.

Garnish with lemon slices and parsley.

Serves: 4

Use left over Béarnaise with steamed broccoli

Preparation: 10 minutes

Cooking: 10 to 15 minutes

Almost Pizza Quiche

This is delicious and fills the pizza craving nicely

4 oz softened cream cheese
4 eggs or 1 cup liquid egg substitute
1/3 cup heavy cream
¼ cup parmesan cheese (grated)
1 Tbsp chives
½ tsp Italian or pizza seasoning
2 cups low fat shredded cheese (*I use mozzarella /cheddar mix*)
½ tsp fresh garlic or 1/4 tsp garlic powder
½ cup lowest carb tomato or pizza sauce
1 cup part skim mozzarella cheese
Toppings to taste
(I use pepperoni, sausage, onion, green pepper,
mushrooms, whatever!)

Beat together cream cheese and eggs till smooth.

Add cream, Parmesan cheese and spices

Spray 13x9 glass baking dish with oil

Put 2 cups of shredded cheese in dish.

Pour egg mixture over all

Bake at 375 for 30 minutes

Spread with sauce and then add your toppings

Cover with mozzarella cheese

Bake till brown and bubbly

Let stand for 5 minutes before cutting.

French Country Supper

Preparation time: 15 minutes;
Cooking time: 5 hours on high; 8 hours on low.

1 to 1½ pounds bone-in skinless chicken thighs
2 tsp dried basil or herbs de Provance
¼ tsp each salt and black pepper
1 small chopped onion medium
4 chopped yellow or orange bell pepper
2 15 to 19-ounce cans rinsed and drained cannellini or
other white beans
1 14½ -ounce can diced tomatoes with, basil, garlic and
oregano or stewed tomatoes with juice

Place chicken in a 4-quart or larger slow cooker.

Sprinkle & with basil or herbs de Provance, salt and
pepper.

Add onion bell pepper, beans and tomatoes.

Cover and cook on high 5 hours or low, 8 hours or until
chicken is no longer pink.

Makes 4 servings.

Yellowfin Tuna Steaks

3 tbsp olive oil
3 oz. light Japanese soy sauce
½ oz. black peppercorns, coarsely ground
2 dried chilies, ground
3 garlic cloves, minced

Marinate tuna 30 minutes.

Grill, using marinade for basting

Use high heat to sear fish on outside while still pink in the center.

Serve with "The Salsa" on the side

Seafood Casserole

1/3 cup Olive Oil
2 cups chopped onions
3 large cloves garlic, chopped
½ -cup juice from canned clams (strain this to make sure there is no grit)
1- 1 lb.12 oz. can stewed tomatoes (with celery, green peppers, and onions)
1-cup tomato sauce (preferably homemade)
1-tsp shrimp base (available at gourmet and specialty shops)
½ tsp oregano
½ tsp basil
¼ tsp pepper

FISH--
2 lbs. Cod or grouper
12 large raw shrimp (16-20 per lb.)
4 tbsp small shrimp, raw
4 tbsp canned chopped clams wash well to be sure there is no grit
8 mussels in shells steamed just until open
1- 2 lb. Spaghetti Squash

Heat oil. Add onions and cook until onions are soft.

Add next 8 ingredients. Simmer for 30 minutes.

Add cod or grouper all shrimp and mussels. Cook just until not quite done. Add clams and allow to heat through

As soon as mussels open serve over spaghetti squash, pouring plenty of sauce over all.

Serves: 4
Preparation: 10 minutes
Cooking: 50 to 60 minutes

Pizza, South Beach Style

3 mini Portabella mushrooms
3 heaping spoonfuls of pizza sauce (be sure to check the sugar content)
low fat mozzarella cheese

Preheat toaster oven or regular oven to 350.

Wash the mushrooms and dry them thoroughly.

Scoop out the stem from the mushroom.

Spoon in some pizza sauce where the stem was removed.

Top with low fat mozzarella cheese and any other pizza topping that you prefer.

Bake until the cheese is melted and browned about 12 minutes.

A dash of red pepper flakes provides a little zip.

Veggies

Fire and Ice Tomatoes

5 large tomatoes, cut into wedges
1 medium onion, sliced
¾ cup white vinegar
6 tbsp Splenda
¼ cup water
1 tbsp mustard seed
¼ tsp cayenne pepper
1 large cucumber, sliced

In a large bowl, combine the tomatoes and onion; set aside.

In a small saucepan, combine the vinegar, Splenda, water, mustard seed and cayenne.

Bring to a boil; boil for 1 minute.

Pour over tomatoes and onion; toss to coat.

Cover and refrigerate for at least 2 hours.

Add cucumber; toss to coat.

Refrigerate overnight.

Serve with a slotted spoon.

Yield: 8 servings.

Green Beans With Red Peppers

¼ pound fresh green beans, trimmed
½ cup julienne sweet red pepper
½ tsp olive or canola oil
1 tsp balsamic vinegar
1/8 to ¼ tsp dried basil
1/8 tsp pepper

In a nonstick skillet coated with nonstick cooking spray, sauté beans and red pepper in oil for 4 minutes or until crisp-tender.

Stir in the vinegar, basil and pepper.

Yield: 2 servings.

Broccoli Brown Rice Pilaf

For 2nd Phase

1 cup raw brown rice
2¼ cups reduced-sodium chicken broth or vegetable broth
2 tbsp minced fresh rosemary or 2 tsp dried rosemary, crushed
2 garlic cloves, minced
2 cups chopped fresh broccoli
¼ cup slivered almonds
¼ cup unsalted sunflower kernels
½ tsp salt
1/8 tsp pepper

In a large nonstick skillet coated with nonstick cooking spray, sauté rice until lightly browned.

Add the broth, rosemary and garlic; bring to a boil.

Reduce heat; cover and simmer for 40 minutes or until rice is almost tender.

Stir in the broccoli, almonds, sunflower kernels, salt and pepper.

Cover and cook 3-5 minutes longer or until rice is tender and broccoli is crisp-tender.

Fluff with a fork.

Yield: 6 servings.

Mediterranean Broccoli Salad

Dressing:
½ cup extra virgin olive oil
¼ cup balsamic vinegar
1/8 tsp oregano
¼ tsp salt 2 cups broccoli florets
1 (4 oz.) can sliced black olives, drained
1 (7 oz.) jar roasted red peppers, drained and diced
½ cup red onions, thinly sliced
1 (4 oz.) package crumbled feta cheese

Combine dressing ingredients in jar or bowl and set aside.

In salad bowl, combine broccoli with all other ingredients.

Whisk together the dressing ingredients and pour over the
vegetables.

Gently stir to combine. Refrigerate until ready to serve.

Serves 8.

Zucchini Casserole

Zucchini
Onion
Green Pepper
sliced tomato
2 percent cheese slices, any flavor
Salt and pepper to taste

Layer each ingredient in ovenproof dish and bake at 350
for 40 minutes.

Cheese Baked Zucchini

4 medium zucchini
2 tbsp extra virgin olive oil
4 oz mozzarella cheese, thinly sliced
2 large tomatoes, seeded & diced
2 Tbsp fresh oregano or basil, chopped

Preheat oven to 400 degrees

Slice zucchini lengthwise into 4 strips each.

Brush with oil and place on cookie sheet lined with parchment paper.

Bake in preheated 400-degree oven for 10 minutes

Remove zucchini from oven.

Arrange slices of cheese on top and sprinkle with diced tomatoes and spice.

Return to oven for 5 minutes or until cheese melts.

Remove from oven and transfer to serving plate.

Serves 4

Stuffed Zucchini With Cheese

4 or 5 med. zucchini
1 lg. onion, chopped
1 clove garlic, chopped
½ c. dried parsley
2 tsp. olive oil
1 tsp. oregano
1 tsp. salt
Pinch of pepper
½ c. Parmesan cheese
3 beaten eggs
¼ c. Whole Grain Cracker crumbs

Wash and cook zucchini whole in very little boiling water for 5 minutes.

Drain and cool.

Cut them in half, lengthwise and hollow out zucchini, leaving 1/4 inch of flesh.

Chop the pulp and sauté in oil with onion, garlic, salt, pepper, cheese, eggs, and most of the Whole Wheat Cracker crumbs

Sprinkle salt on hollowed out zucchini and fill with stuffing

Sprinkle with remainder of the Whole Grain Cracker crumbs and place in baking dish.

Cover and bake for 45 minutes at 350 degrees.

Serve with tomato sauce or as is.

Baked Brussels Sprouts

2½ lb. Brussels sprouts or 3 pkg. (10 oz. each) frozen
Brussels Sprouts
Boiling, salted water
6 slices turkey bacon, diced
¼ cup olive oil
½ cup finely chopped onion
1½ cup heavy cream
1/3 cup chicken broth
½ tsp. each salt and oregano leaves
¾ tsp dill weed, crumbled
1/8 tsp pepper

Wash fresh sprouts thoroughly and trim off stem ends.

Cut an X into each stem end.

Cook, uncovered, in a large quantity of boiling water until just tender when pierced, 7 to 10 minutes. (Or cook frozen Brussels sprouts in boiling water or microwave as directed on package).

Drain well and arrange in a shallow 2-quart casserole.

Meanwhile in a sauté pan, cook bacon over medium heat until crisp with olive oil; lift out with a slotted spoon, drain and set aside.

Discard all but 2 tbsp of the drippings.

Add the onion to the drippings and cook until limp.

Gradually stir in the cream.

Cook, stirring, until it boils and thickens.

Add the chicken broth, salt, oregano, dill, pepper and all but 2 tbsp of the cooked bacon.

Pour sauce evenly over the Brussels sprouts.

Sprinkle remaining bacon over top.

Cover and refrigerate if made ahead.

Bake, uncovered in a 325-degree oven for 20 minutes (35 minutes if refrigerated) or until heated through. Makes 8 to 10 servings.

Meet the Spaghetti Squash

Averaging from 4 to 8 pounds, the cylinder shaped spaghetti squash is generally available year-round with a peak season from early fall through winter. While a true spaghetti squash is pale ivory to pale yellow in color, in the early 1990's, an orange spaghetti squash, known as "Orangetti" was developed and this is what is frequently found in today's supermarkets. Higher in beta carotene, the orange variety is also bit sweeter than its paler counterpart, although both have a mild flavor that is easily enhanced by the food served with or on it. A dieter's dream, a four-ounce serving of spaghetti squash has only 37 calories.

Buying & Storing

When buying spaghetti squash, look for hard fruit that is heavy for its size, about eight to nine inches in length and four to five inches in diameter and with a pale even color. Avoid any squash with soft spots and green color is a sign of immaturity. The average four-pound spaghetti squash will yield about five cups.

Spaghetti Squash can be stored at room temperature for about a month. After cutting, wrap in plastic wrap and refrigerate up to 2 days. Spaghetti squash also freezes well. Pack cooked squash into freezer bags, seal, label and freeze. Partially thaw before re-using, and then steam until tender but still firm, about 5 minutes.

How To Cook Spaghetti Squash

- **Bake It** -- Pierce the whole shell several times with a large fork or skewer and place in baking dish.

Cook squash in preheated 375°F oven approximately 1 hour or until flesh is tender.

- **Boil It** -- Heat a pot of water large enough to hold the whole squash. When the water is boiling, drop in the squash and cook for 20 to 30 minutes, depending on its size. When a fork goes easily into the flesh, the squash is done.
- **Microwave It** -- Cut squash in half lengthwise; remove seeds. Place squash cut sides up in a microwave dish with ¼ cup water. Cover with plastic wrap and cook on high for 10 to 12 minutes, depending on size of squash. Add more cooking time if necessary. Let stand covered, for 5 minutes. With fork "comb" out the strands.
- **Slow Cooker or Crock-Pot** - Choose a smaller spaghetti squash (unless you have an extra large slow cooker) so that it will fit. Add 2 cups of water to slow cooker. Pierce the whole shell several times with a large fork or skewer, add to Crock Pot, cover and cook on low for 8 to 9 hours.

Once the squash is cooked, let it cool for 10 to 20 minutes so it will be easier to handle, before cutting in half (if it wasn't already) and removing the seeds. Pull a fork lengthwise through the flesh to separate it into long strands. You can do these steps ahead of time, and then prepare any of the spaghetti squash recipes whenever the mood strikes.

Spaghetti Squash with Vegetables & Mozzarella

1 spaghetti squash, cooked by your favorite method and separated into strands
1 lg. yellow onion, diced
1 green bell pepper, chopped
1 red bell pepper, chopped
2 T olive oil
1 can (28 oz.) crushed tomatoes
3-5 cloves garlic, minced
1 tsp. basil
½ tsp. oregano
½ tsp. crushed red pepper (optional)
1 Cup grated mozzarella cheese
½ Cup grated Parmesan cheese

Preheat oven to 375 F. Mix the cheese together, set aside.

Heat olive oil in a skillet and add the onion, pepper and garlic.

Sauté over medium heat for about 5 minutes.

Add crushed tomatoes, basil, and crushed red pepper (if using).

Simmer uncovered for about 15 minutes.

Mix squash well with the cooked vegetables and put half in the bottom of a large (13 x 9 inch) baking dish.

Top with half the cheese mixture, followed by the other half of the squash mixture, then the rest of the cheese.

81

Bake for 30 minutes, or until cheese is bubbly and slightly browned.

Let cool 10-15 minutes before serving.

Serves 6-8

Spaghetti Squash Alfredo

1 med spaghetti squash, cooked by your favorite method
and separated into strands
1 Cup fat free sour cream
½ Cup shredded mozzarella cheese
¼ Cup grated Parmesan cheese
2 cloves garlic, finely minced
¼ tsp. salt
¼ tsp. black pepper

In a medium-sized saucepan, combine the all ingredients
except spaghetti squash over medium-low heat

Whisk until smooth and creamy, stirring constantly to
prevent burning.

Add the spaghetti squash strands to the sauce and stir
until thoroughly mixed and heated through.

Serve immediately.

Serves 6-8

Spaghetti Squash Pancakes

6 Cups spaghetti squash, cooked by your favorite method
and separated into strands
1/3 Cup all-purpose flour
½ Cup grated Parmesan cheese
4 Tbsp butter or olive oil
salt and pepper to taste
sour cream and apple sauce for garnish

Add flour & cheese to the strands of the cooked spaghetti
squash.

Mix well, using two forks.

Depending on the flavor you wish, or your dietary
preferences, melt 1 tbsp butter in a large skillet over
medium-high heat or heat olive oil in skillet instead.

Spoon 1/4 cup squash mixture into prepared skillet.

With a fork, press to form an evenly thick cake.

Repeat to fill skillet.

Cook cakes until bottoms are lightly browned, turn over
and brown second side.

Continue until you've used all the squash mixture

Keep the cakes already made warm in an oven set at its
lowest temperature until you are ready to serve.

Use additional butter or oil as necessary for cooking.

Sprinkle pancakes with salt and pepper and serve with sour cream and/or applesauce.

Serves 6-8 as a side dish or appetizer

Low Carb Spaghetti Squash Pancakes

6 Cups spaghetti squash, cooked by your favorite method
and separated into strands
4 eggs
2 Tbsp chopped green onion or chives
salt and pepper to taste
oil for skillet

Add eggs, onion or chives, salt and pepper to cooked
spaghetti squash.

Form into 3-inch patties.

Heat oil in a skillet and cook for 3-4 minutes on each side.

For a different flavor, you can sauté the patties in butter.

For an Asian flair, sauté in canola oil mixed with a few
drops of sesame oil, serve with soy sauce.

Makes About 30 Patties

Spaghetti Squash Frittata

1 Cup spaghetti squash, cooked by your favorite method
and separated into strands
4 eggs, lightly beaten
2 Tbsp chopped Italian parsley
3 Tbsp grated Parmesan cheese
1 Cup finely chopped red onion
3-4 garlic cloves, minced
½ tsp. salt
½ tsp. pepper
1/8 tsp. cayenne
1 Tbsp butter

Preheat broiler.

Combine all ingredients in a large mixing bowl.

Melt butter in a large skillet.

Pour mixture into the skillet and cook over low heat for
about 12-15 minutes.

Place under to broiler for 2 to 3 minutes or until top is
browned

Serves 6

Spicy Chicken (or Turkey) & Spaghetti Squash Skillet

1 small spaghetti squash, cooked by your favorite method
and separated into strands
2 Tbsp olive oil
½ Cup minced onion
3-4 cloves garlic, minced
2 green onions, finely chopped
12 oz. cooked chicken or turkey meat
2 Cup canned crushed tomatoes
¼ Cup dry red wine
2 tsp. capers
2½ tsp. fresh oregano (1 tsp. dried)
1 tsp. crushed red pepper, or more to taste
3 Tbsp Italian parsley, finely chopped

Heat the oil in a skillet over medium high heat

Sauté onion, garlic and green onions for 2 minutes.

Add the chicken or turkey and cook for about 3-4 minutes.

Stir in tomatoes and wine and bring to a boil, then lower heat and simmer for about 20 minutes.

Add remaining ingredients and simmer for another 5 minutes.

Pour sauce over heated spaghetti squash and serve.

Serves 6

Pesto Spaghetti Squash with Mozzarella

1 spaghetti squash, cooked by your favorite method and separated into strands
1 Tbsp olive oil
¾ Cup pesto sauce (see sauces)
4 oz smoked or plain mozzarella cheese, shredded
¼ Cup grated Parmesan cheese

Heat oil in a large skillet over medium high heat

Add spaghetti squash.

Using two forks to lift, mix in pesto.

Cook just long enough to heat through,

Mix in cheeses, heat until everything is well mixed and cheese is beginning to melt.

Serve immediately

Serves 6 to 8 as a side dish

Middle Eastern Style Spaghetti Squash

1 spaghetti squash, cooked by your favorite method and separated into strands
2 Tbsp butter
2 Tbsp olive oil
½ tsp. ground cardamom
¾ tsp. ground coriander
1/8 tsp. ground ginger
1/8 tsp. allspice
salt & white pepper to taste
½ Cup toasted slivered almonds
zest of 1 orange

In a large skillet over medium heat, heat butter and oil then stir in spices, except salt and pepper.

Cook for about a minute.

Stir in squash and sauté until well coated, adding white pepper and salt to taste.

Remove to serving dish.

Sprinkle with toasted almonds and orange zest just before serving

Serves 6 to 8 as a side dish

Spaghetti Squash Chicken Alfredo

4 boneless chicken breasts cut into bite size pieces
4 Tbsp butter
1 med spaghetti squash, cooked by your favorite method
and separated into strands
½ Cup heavy cream
½ Cup shredded Parmesan cheese
½ Cup shredded mozzarella cheese

Sauté chicken pieces in butter until cooked, about 10 minutes.

Heat cream on the stove and when it is very warm, add the cheese and stir to melt.

Combine the cheese sauce with the cooked pieces of chicken and the cooked spaghetti squash strands.

Sprinkle with extra Parmesan cheese if desired.

Serves 4

Oysters and Spaghetti Squash

24 shucked oysters
1 large spaghetti squash
8 tbsp butter
salt and freshly ground pepper
1½ Cup heavy cream
pinch of nutmeg
¼ Cup grated Parmiggano-Reggiano cheese
1 Cup finely chopped fresh herbs like parsley, chives, basil, chervil
cayenne pepper to taste

Preheat oven to 350° F.

Cut squash in half, remove seeds and stringy center, season with salt and pepper and bake, cut side down, in a pan filled with about an inch of water.

It is done when it separates into strands but is not mushy.

When cool enough to handle, comb out the long strands of flesh with a fork.

Place in a heatproof dish; mix with 4 tbsp of butter, season, cover and reheat in the oven before serving.

Remove the oysters from the shells and pat dry.

Combine cream, remaining butter and nutmeg in a heavy saucepan and boil over medium heat until the sauce is reduced to about 1 cup.

Remove from heat and whisk in the cheese until it melts.

Stir in the fresh herbs and oysters and cook over low heat until the edge of the oysters start to curl.

Season to taste.

Arrange the hot squash on a serving platter, pour the sauce over it and serve immediately.

Serves 6

Asparagus with Sesame-Ginger Sauce

1 tbsp. soy sauce
1 tbsp. rice vinegar
1 tbsp. peanut oil
1 tbsp. water
1 tbsp. Tahini (pureed sesame seeds)
1 tsp. chopped fresh ginger
1/2 tsp. chopped garlic
1 tbsp. SPLENDA®
Pinch red pepper flakes
48 medium-size asparagus spears trimmed, peeled and cleaned

In a food processor, combine everything except the asparagus and mix until thoroughly blended. Set aside.

Cut the asparagus into two-inch pieces, on the diagonal.

Half fill large skillet with water, cover and bring to a boil. Add the asparagus and simmer just until crisp-tender, approximately four to five minutes. Drain well,

but do not rinse.

Transfer to serving bowl. Pour the sauce over the hot asparagus and toss to coat. Serve warm or at room temperature.

7 servings (2/3 cup 4.3 oz.)

Broccoli with Garlic Sauce

1 large bunch fresh broccoli,
1 bunch scallions (6-7)
3 large cloves garlic
¼ cup beef broth
1 tbsp. low-sodium soy sauce (40 percent less salt)
1 tbsp. cornstarch
1 tsp. SPLENDA® Granular
1 tbsp. minced cilantro
½ tsp. sesame oil

Trim broccoli and cut into florets (retain about 60% of the bunch). Rinse broccoli, shake off excess water and place in 3-quart microwave-safe casserole dish. Set aside.

Slice white scallion bulbs into rings and mince garlic. Stir together scallions, garlic, beef broth, soy sauce, cornstarch, SPLENDA® Granular and cilantro.

Pour sauce over broccoli, cover and microwave on high for 4 minutes.

Stir broccoli, replace cover, and microwave on high for 3 minutes or until broccoli is desired texture and sauce has thickened to coat broccoli. Stir in sesame oil and serve hot.

Serves: 4

Chinese Green Beans

1 16-oz. package frozen green beans
½ tsp chicken base
1 bunch scallion (6-7)
2 large cloves of garlic
½ tsp. ground ginger
1 tsp. Soy sauce, low sodium
1 tsp. SPLENDA®
1 tbsp. creamy peanut butter
1/8 tsp. sesame oil

In a 2-quart microwave-safe casserole dish, combine green beans and chicken base. Cover and microwave on high for 4 minutes.

Meanwhile, slice white bulbs of scallions into rings and mince garlic.

In small bowl, combine ginger, soy sauce and SPLENDA® Granular. Add scallion rings and garlic. Set aside.

Remove green beans from microwave and uncover. Pour sauce over beans and stir. Cover and microwave on high for 4 minutes.

Stir in peanut butter and sesame oil until sauce coats the beans and serve immediately

Serves: 6

Dilly Beans

3 tbsp. olive oil
¾ cup white wine vinegar
1 tsp. SPLENDA® Granular
3 tbsp. minced fresh dill
1½ lb. green beans, trimmed and rinsed

In a large bowl, whisk together the oil, vinegar, SPLENDA® Granular and dill. Set aside.

Bring a large pot of water to a boil and parboil the green beans until crisp-tender, approximately three minutes, depending on size of beans.

Drain well.

Add the beans to the bowl of dressing, tossing and stirring to coat the beans.

Add salt and pepper to taste, and then let the beans come to room temperature, stirring occasionally.

Serve immediately or refrigerate until needed.

Serves: 6

Stir-Fried Green Beans

Stir-Fry Sauce
1 ½ tbsp. minced garlic
1 ½ tbsp. minced fresh ginger
2 scallions (white and green parts) minced
2 tbsp. dry sherry
2 tbsp. SPLENDA® Granular
2 tbsp. soy sauce
1 tbsp. water
2 tbsp. peanut oil or oil

Combine the Stir-Fry Sauce ingredients in a small bowl.
Set aside.

Stir-Fry
1 ½ lb. green beans, trimmed, and rinsed
2 tbsp. Water

In a large skillet or wok, heat the oil and stir-fry the green
beans until they are barely crisp-tender, approximately 2
minutes.

Add the water and continue stir-frying for another two
minutes, until the beans are crisp-tender and water has
evaporated.

Add the sauce and continue stir-frying for five or six more
minutes, until the beans are tender but not overcooked.
Serve immediately.

Serves: 6

Salads

Cottage Tuna Salad

1 6 oz. can water packed tuna
1 cup low-fat cottage cheese
2 hard-boiled eggs -- peeled and chopped
¼ cup minced celery
¼ cup minced green onion
¼ cup minced dill pickle
1 tsp lemon pepper seasoning
¼ tsp salt
1 Tbsp. low fat mayonnaise

Mix all ingredients together, chill and serve on a bed of mixed greens.

Makes two servings

Cottage Shrimp Salad

5 oz boiled tiny shrimp
1 cup low-fat cottage cheese
2 hard-boiled eggs- peeled and chopped
¼ cup minced celery
¼ cup minced green onion
¼ cup minced dill pickle
1 tsp Old Bay seasoning
¼ tsp salt
1 Tbsp. low fat mayonnaise

Mix ingredients together and chill. Makes about 2 1/2 cups or two servings.

White Bean And Sausage Salad

1 package (12 oz) low-fat Italian turkey sausage links, cut into thin slices

¼ cup balsamic vinegar

2 Tbsp Dijon mustard

1 Tbsp olive oil

2 cans (16 oz ea) cannellini (or other small white beans) beans, rinsed and drained

2 red bell peppers cut into 1-in. cubes

1 large red onion, diced

1/4 c minced fresh parsley

pepper (to taste)

1 bag (10 oz) lettuce mix

In a large nonstick sauté pan, sauté sausage slices 8 minutes, until cooked through.

1n a large bowl, whisk together vinegar and mustard. Whisk 1n oil. Stir in beans, red peppers, onions, parsley, and pepper.

Add sausage and toss well. (Make ahead and refrigerate to blend flavors)

Place lettuce on individual plates and top with salad. Serve at room temperature.

Serves 6

Cucumber Salad

1 sm. pkg. Sugar free lemon gelatin
1 cup grated cucumber, peel included
2 Tbsp grated onion
1 cup low fat mayonnaise
1 Tbsp lemon juice

Dissolve gelatin in one and one half cups boiling water.

Add the lemon juice.

When partially set add the other ingredients.

Stir well and chill until completely set.

Tomato, Cucumber, and Feta Salad

2 tomatoes, cored and sliced
1½ cucumbers, peeled, seeded and sliced
Salt and pepper
2 tbsp red wine vinegar
3 tbsp olive oil
1/2 cup feta cheese, crumbled

In medium bowl combine tomatoes and cucumber.

Season with salt and pepper.

Add vinegar and olive oil.

Toss to coat.

Sprinkle on feta and serve.

Serves 4

Tomato Mozzarella Salad

¼ cup olive oil
2 tbsp vinegar
1 tbsp fresh parsley, chopped
2 tsp Dijon mustard
1 tsp Splenda
2 cloves garlic, minced
½ tsp dried basil
½ tsp black pepper
¼ tsp salt
2 tbsp water
3 large tomatoes, very ripe
16 romaine lettuce leaves
½ cup mozzarella cheese, cubed
6 green onions, sliced

Vinaigrette: In a jar with tight fitting lid; whisk together oil, vinegar, parsley, mustard, sugar, garlic, basil, pepper, salt and water; chill.

Shake before using.

Salad: Cut tomatoes in half; cut each half crosswise into slices.
Arrange 2 lettuce leaves on 8 salad plates.

Arrange tomatoes slices on lettuce; sprinkle with cheese and green onion.

At serving time, pour vinaigrette over each salad.

Serves 8

Rice Salad

¾ cup raw brown rice
2 tsp olive oil
2 tbsp chicken broth from poached chicken
1 tsp dried tarragon
1-cup cucumber cubes
Salt and freshly ground black pepper

Bring a 3- to 4-quart sauce- pan filled with water to a boil.

Add the rice and boil according to package directions.

Drain and toss with olive oil and chicken broth.

Add tarragon and cucumber and mix well.

Add salt and pepper to taste.

Makes 2 servings

Creamy Cole Slaw

1½ cups Hellmann's® Low Fat Mayonnaise
1/3 cup SPLENDA® Granular
3 Tbsp. Vidalia Onion, (or other sweet onion) finely
chopped
2 tsp. Lemon Juice
1 Tbsp. White Wine Vinegar
1¼ tsp. Celery Seed
¾ tsp. Salt
¼ tsp. Black Pepper
8 cups Classic Cole Slaw Cabbage Mix (1 Bag)

Whisk all ingredients except cabbage
mix and carrots in large bowl.

Add Cole slaw mix.

Refrigerate for at least two hours.

Mix and serve cold.

Warm Spinach Salad

1-7 oz bag Baby Spinach Greens
¼ Cup White Vinegar
¼ Cup Water
¼ Cup Dijon Mustard
3 Tbsp. SPLENDA® Granular
5 Slices Turkey Bacon
¼ Cup Chopped Red Onion
2 cloves Garlic, minced

Place spinach greens in a bowl.

Remove any undesirable leaves or large stems.

Blend together vinegar, water, mustard and SPLENDA®

Add to bacon mixture. Set aside.

Finely slice bacon into small strips.

Place in a medium sized sauté pan and fry over medium high heat until crispy (approx. 3-4 minutes).

Add onion and garlic and cook over medium high heat for 1-2 minutes.

Add vinegar mixture and simmer 1-2 minutes.

Pour over spinach.

Toss well. Serve immediately.

Makes 4 Servings

Danish Cucumber Salad

4 Cucumbers, medium sized
2 tsp. Salt
½ Cup White Vinegar
¼ Cup SPLENDA®
2 Tbsp. Chopped, Fresh Dill
¼ tsp. White Pepper

Cut cucumbers into paper-thin slices. Toss with salt.
Marinate with 2 tsp. salt at room temperature 1 hour.

Drain liquid from cucumber. Add remaining ingredients.
Stir. Cover and refrigerate 3 hours before serving

10 servings

Raw Broccoli Salad

4 cups Broccoli Florets or Broccolini
¼ cup Red Onion, minced
2 Tbsp. SPLENDA® Granular
2 Tbsp. Cider Vinegar
2 Tbsp. Light Mayonnaise
2 Tbsp. Sunflower Seeds shelled, roasted and salted

Finely chop florets or Broccolini. Set aside.

Place remaining ingredients in a medium-sized mixing bowl. Mix well.

Add broccoli florets or Broccolini. Toss until coated.

Chill until ready to serve.

6 servings

Layered Chinese Chicken Salad

Because of the cornstarch and the mandarin oranges, this is a phase 2 or 3 dish

Dressing
½ cup SPLENDA® Granular
2-3 Tbsp. Chinese Chile Garlic Paste (Olek Sambal)
1/3 cup Light Mayonnaise
3 tsp. Fresh Ginger, minced
¼ cup Light Soy Sauce
¾ cup Rice Vinegar
1¾ tsp. Cornstarch
1/3 cup Water

Salad
4 Boneless, Skinless Chicken Breasts
1 cup Snow Peas, trimmed and halved
1-15 oz. can Mandarin Oranges, drained
2-12 oz. bags Asian Slaw Mix

Garnish
1/3 cup Chopped Green Onion
1 cup Toasted Sliced Almonds

Mix SPLENDA® Granular, chili garlic paste, light mayonnaise and ginger together in a medium mixing bowl. Stir well. Add soy sauce and rice vinegar. Mix until well blended.

Pour 1/4 cup of dressing in a small bowl. Place chicken breasts in bowl, tossing to coat. Marinate in refrigerator 45-60 minutes.

Place remaining dressing in a small saucepan. Set aside. Mix together cornstarch and water in a small bowl until cornstarch is dissolved. Pour cornstarch mixture into dressing while stirring constantly. Place pan on medium-high heat. Boil dressing over medium-high heat approx. 2 minutes, while stirring constantly. Remove dressing from heat and pour into a small bowl. Refrigerate at least 1 hour or until cool.

Remove marinated chicken breasts from refrigerator. Grill or broil chicken until internal temperature reaches 160°F. Set aside to cool. Slice thinly or shred cooled breasts. Cover and refrigerate until ready to use.

Assembly:

Place 1 bag (8 cups) of Asian Slaw in a straight-sided glass bowl. Drizzle a third of the prepared dressing over the slaw. Arrange 1/2 of the sliced or shredded chicken breasts and pea pods on top of the slaw mix.

Pour remaining slaw into bowl. Top with remaining chicken and oranges. Pour remaining dressing over the salad. Refrigerate until ready to serve.

Just before serving top with sliced almonds and green onion.

Options:

For a more "authentic Asian" flavor add 1-2 tsp. toasted sesame oil.

13 (1 cup) servings

Snacks

Mock Hummus

1 can White Kidney Beans, (try black beans) rinsed and
drained (I use Great Northern without the pork)
2 cloves garlic
1½ Tbsp olive oil
4 sprigs fresh mint leaves or dried to taste
6 sprigs fresh thyme leaves or dried to taste
salt and black pepper to taste
3 Tbsp chives, chopped

Pulse all ingredients except chives in food processor until a
smooth paste forms.

If too thick, thin it down with lemon juice until you reach
the desired consistency similar to hummus.

The lemon juice also gives it a nice Mediterranean kick.

Garnish with chives.

Serve with celery or sliced zucchini.

Mexican Deviled Eggs

8 hard cooked eggs, peeled
½ cup shredded cheddar (use Fat Free)
¼ cup mayo (use low fat or Fat Free)
¼ cup drained salsa
2 Tbsp sliced green onions
1 Tbsp sour cream
Salt to taste

Slice eggs in half lengthwise.

Remove yolks, set whites aside.

In a bowl, mash yolks with cheese, salsa, mayo, onions, sour cream and salt.

Divide the filling among the egg whites.

Serve immediately or chill until ready to serve.

Sprinkle with a little paprika to garnish.

Deviled Eggs

4 hard-boiled eggs
1 small avocado
1 tsp chopped green olives w/pimentos
pepper
paprika

Boil the eggs, peel and let cool;

Slice the eggs, putting the white halves in serving dish.

Cut the avocado into chunks; squeeze lemon juice on the avocado to keep the slices green;

Season with pepper;

Add the avocado chunks to the yellows
with a fork mash until fairly smooth,

Add olives, stir and mash until the proper consistency has been reached,

Spoon this mix into the egg whites;

Garnish with a sprinkle of paprika!

Smoked Salmon Pate

1 8 oz. package of low-fat cream cheese (softened)
1 7 oz. can of salmon (drained)
1 tbsp. of minced onions
1 tsp. lemon juice
1 tsp. liquid smoke

Combine all ingredients in a bowl.

Stir with a fork until blended.

Chill 2 - 3 hours.

Serve with celery sticks.

On Phase 2 or 3 can be used on whole-wheat crackers. (Go to the natural grocery store in your area and buy real whole-wheat crackers. No white flour)

Cheese Crisp

Spray a microwave safe plate with butter flavor cooking spray.

Place a slice of low fat or 2 percent cheese on the plate.

Microwave it for approx. 1 1/2 min. or until you can scrape it loose with a knife.

Eat this like potato chips, or add any topping and enjoy.

Ham and turkey work well, and taco type things are a real treat. Use your imagination.

Hamburger Bean Deep

2 lbs. ground round, very lean
1 lg. can refried beans (vegetarian style)
1 lg. bottle salsa
1 sm. bottle hot salsa
1 sm. can diced chilies
1 green pepper
½ cup diced onion

Brown ground beef, drain well and add remaining ingredients.

Simmer about 10 minutes.

Serve as dip with slices of raw vegetables

Molded Salmon Appetizer

2 envelopes unflavored gelatin
¼ cup cold water
½ cup boiling fish stock
1-cup cool fish stock
1 tsp Worcestershire Sauce
8 oz smoked salmon or for a real treat use some left over grilled salmon from another meal
1 cup finely chopped celery
½ cup finely chopped green onions
½ cup low fat mayonnaise
2 tsp Dijon Mustard
½ cup heavy cream, whipped

Sprinkle gelatin on cold water and allow to stand until softened. Stir in the hot stock and make sure the gelatin is dissolved. Add Worchester, salt & pepper to taste. Add remaining ingredients, except whipped cream. Place in a food processor and blend well. Fold in whipped cream. Pour into oiled 5-cup mold. Refrigerate until firm, a minimum of six hours. Serve with fresh vegetables and whole grain crackers.

Fancy Spiced Nuts

1 egg white
2 tbsp cold-water
¼ pound shelled nuts
½ cup granulated Splenda
1/8 tsp salt
1½ tsp cinnamon
½ tsp allspice
1/3 tsp ginger
1/3 tsp nutmeg

Beat lightly the egg white and cold water.

Dip nutmeats into the egg white mixture.

Combine all dry ingredients in a separate bowl.

Drop nutmeats one at a time into dry mixture and roll about lightly.

Keep nuts separated.

Place on cookie sheet and bake at 250 degrees F for at least one hour.

Remove from oven and shake off excess sugar and spice mixture.

Store tightly covered.

Teriyaki Almonds

2 cups almonds
1 tsp lemon juice
1 tbsp olive oil
½ tsp salt
¼ tsp onion powder
1 tbsp soy sauce
1 tsp brown Splenda
½ tsp ginger
¼ tsp garlic powder

Preheat oven to 325 degrees F.

Place nuts in a 13 x 9-inch baking pan.

Bake for 5 minutes.

In a bowl, combine soy sauce, lemon juice and brown sugar.

Stir until Splenda is dissolved.

Stir in oil, ginger, salt, garlic and onion powder.

Add heated almonds.

Toss to coat nuts.

Return nuts to baking pan.

Bake 10 minutes longer, turning once.

Cool and store in an airtight container.

Oriental Almonds

1 ½ tbsp butter or margarine
1 ½ tbsp Worcestershire sauce
1 tsp salt
¼ tsp cinnamon
1/8 tsp chili powder
Dash of hot pepper sauce
1 (10 ounce) package Blue Diamond Whole Almonds (2 cups)

Melt butter in 2-quart baking dish in a 300 degrees F oven.

Stir in Worcestershire sauce, salt, cinnamon, chili powder and hot pepper sauce.

Add almonds; stir until completely coated.

Bake, stirring occasionally, 15 minutes or until almonds are crisp.

Makes 2 cups.

Smoked Almonds

½ tsp liquid smoke
2 tsp water
1 ½ cups shelled, skin on almonds
2 tsp butter or margarine
½ tsp salt (more, if needed)

Mix together liquid smoke and water; pour over almonds and mix to cover all almonds.

Place in shallow Pyrex pan; cover and let stand overnight.

The next day heat almonds in 300-degree oven.

When they are warm, add about 1 tsp butter.

Toss to coat almonds, adding more butter if necessary.

Roast for 40 to 45 minutes, stirring frequently. Sprinkle with salt to taste.

Cool and store in a covered container.

Tabasco Almonds

2 cups raw whole almonds, skin-on
2 tbsp unsalted butter, melted
2 tbsp Tabasco sauce (any variety)
2 tsp Worcestershire sauce
1 tsp garlic powder
½ tsp dry mustard
½ tsp cayenne pepper
1½ tsp kosher salt

Preheat oven to 250 degrees F. Line a cookie sheet with parchment paper.

Place all the ingredients except the salt in a large bowl and toss until the nuts are well coated.

Transfer nuts to a cookie sheet lined with parchment and arrange in a single layer.

Bake, stirring every 15 minutes, until the nuts are darkened but not burnt - about 45 minutes.

Remove from oven and immediately loosen the nuts from parchment with a metal spatula.

Little Devils

2 tbsp peanut oil
2 garlic cloves, minced
3 tsp chili powder
2 to 3 tsp ground dried red chilies
1 tsp salt, or more, to taste
1-pound (3 cups) raw peanuts

Preheat oven to 350 degrees F.

In a heavy skillet, warm the oil over low heat.

Add the garlic, and sauté it briefly until it has softened.

Stir in the chili powder, chilies and salt, and mix well.

Sprinkle in the peanuts, and stir to coat them.

Transfer the peanuts to a baking sheet. Bake them 10 minutes, or until they are lightly browned.

Transfer them to absorbent paper.

Let them cool before serving.

Stored in a closed jar, the peanuts will keep several weeks.

Spinach-Feta Cheese Dip

2 cups low-fat plain yogurt
1 small clove garlic
2 tbsp chopped fresh dill or: 2 tsp dried
1 package (9 or 10 ounces) frozen leaf spinach, thawed in
microwave about 5 minutes, squeeze out excess liquid
4 ounces low fat feta cheese, cut into cubes
1 tsp grated lemon rind 1/4 tsp pepper

Set coffee filter or double thickness of paper toweling in
strainer over small bowl.

Spoon yogurt into filter.

Refrigerate and drain for 2 hours. (Yield is about 11/3
cups.)

Chop the garlic and dill in a food processor.

Add spinach, feta, rind, salt and pepper.

Process until cheese is finely grated, scraping down side of
bowl as needed.

Add drained yogurt.

Mix with on/off motion just until mixture is combined.

Scrape into serving bowl. (Can be prepared a day ahead
and refrigerated.)

Black Bean Dip ala Stuart

1 red bell pepper
1 package or bunch cilantro
4 scallions, rough cut
2 Tbsp Lime Juice
2 Tbsp Balsamic
2 Tbsp Hot Pepper Sauce
½ tsp ground allspice
½ tsp ground cumin
¼ tsp salt
¼ tsp black pepper
2 15 oz cans Black Beans
1 Jalapeno pepper
3 cloves garlic

Cut red bell pepper in chunks discarding the stem and seeds.

Place in food processor with remaining ingredients and process until nearly smooth.

Serve with fresh vegetables to dip.

Sauces, Soups and Marinades

Aioli

1 large egg, at room temp
1 Tbsp fresh lemon juice
1 cup olive oil
½ tsp salt
1/8 tsp pepper
1/8 tsp cayenne
1 clove garlic mashed very fine

Combine egg, lemon juice and garlic in a food processor or blender and process for 10 seconds.

With the processor running, slowly pour in the oil.

Stop once the mixture has thickened.

Add the salt, black pepper, and cayenne, and pulse once or twice to blend.

Transfer to an airtight container and refrigerate for at least 30 minutes before using.

Oriental Marinade

2 Tbsp fresh lemon juice
2 Tbsp soy sauce
1 clove garlic, minced
½ tsp Splenda
2 tsp coarsely ground pepper

Mix all ingredients together except pepper.

Put into Ziploc bag and add 1# fresh salmon.

Refrigerate for 30 minutes to 1 hour.

Take out, drain off and discard marinade.

Cover fish with ground pepper and press into fish.

Pat the salmon dry with a paper towel.

Grill.

Bar-B-Q Sauce

Makes 4 Cups (32 oz)
Preparation Time 45 minutes
One serving is ¾ oz
Best if refrigerated overnight before using

1 Tbsp Canola or Extra Virgin Olive Oil
1 cup Onion, minced
2 Garlic Cloves, minced
2 Beef Bouillon Cubes
½ cup Hot Water
3 (6oz.) cans Tomato Paste, divided
1 cup SPLENDA® Granular
¾ cup Worcestershire Sauce
¾ cup Dijon Mustard
3 Tbsp Liquid Smoke, hickory flavored
1 tsp Salt
½ cup Cider Vinegar
1 Tbsp Tabasco (+ 1 tsp. for spicier sauce)

Place oil in a large saucepan.

Add onions and garlic.

Sauté over medium heat until translucent (approx 2-3 min.).

Mix the bouillon and water until partially dissolved.

Add bouillon mixture and all remaining ingredients to the saucepan.

Stir well using a wire whisk.

Simmer, uncovered, 25-30 min. to allow flavors to meld. Stir frequently as it cooks.

Refrigerate overnight in a non-metallic container.

Sauce is best if prepared a day before using.

Keeps well, refrigerated, for 1 week.

Simple Pesto

1 cup chopped basil leaves, packed tightly
3 cloves garlic
½ cup grated parmesan (grate it yourself and use Loccatelli
brand, it really makes a difference)
½ cup pine nuts or walnuts
1 cup good quality olive oil

put basil, garlic, parmesan and nuts in food processor.

Blend until thoroughly pureed

Slowly add oil while blender is running.

Citrus Salsa

6-8 ripe plum tomatoes (blanched, peeled and chopped)
1 medium onion finely chopped
3 cloves of garlic (or to taste) finely minced
1 orange, peeled, seeded and chopped fine
¼ cup of white vinegar
¼ cup of fresh lemon or lime juice (or a combo of both)
pinch of lemon or lime zest
chopped jalapenos to taste -
4 tbsp of chopped cilantro

Mix all ingredients well ahead of serving time (preferably the night before) and refrigerate.

Picante Sauce

1 10.75-ounce can tomato puree
1 can full of water (1 1/3 cups)
1/3 cup chopped Spanish onion
1-2 chopped fresh jalapeno peppers, with seeds
2 tbsp white vinegar
rounded ¼ tsp salt
½ small onion minced
2 cloves garlic minced

1. Combine all ingredients in a saucepan over medium/high heat.

2. Bring to a boil then reduce heat and simmer for 30 minutes or until thick.

3. When cool, bottle in 16-ounce jar and refrigerate overnight.

Makes 2 cups (16 oz.).

Note:
For the mild version of this sauce, reduce the amount of fresh jalapenos to 1 rounded tbsp.

For the hot variety, increase the amount of jalapenos to 3-4

Classic Vinaigrette Recipe

1 tsp. Dijon mustard
2 tbsp. red wine vinegar
1 tsp. lemon juice
¼ tsp. salt
¼ c. olive oil
4-5 twists of a pepper mill

Combine ingredients and whisk. Makes 3 or 4 servings.

Italian Dressing

Preparation Time: 2-3 minutes
Serving Size: 2 Tbsp
Serves: 8

½ cup canola or olive oil
¼ cup white wine vinegar
2 tsp. dried basil
1 ½ tsp. salt
1 tsp. SPLENDA® Granular
½ tsp. garlic powder
1 tbsp. light mayonnaise (half the calories)
3 tbsp. Water

Combine all ingredients in a blender.

Blend on high until combined, approximately 30 seconds.

Pour into small pitcher or dressing cruet.

Cover and chill until ready to serve.

Shake or stir before pouring.

Spicy Peanut Sauce

Preparation Time: 5 minutes
Serving Size: 2 Tbsp
Serves: 12

½ cup chunky or smooth peanut butter
2 garlic cloves, quartered
1 tbsp. coarsely chopped fresh ginger
1 small fresh hot pepper, cleaned, and diced
¼ cup peanut oil
2 tbsp. soy sauce
2 tbsp. SPLENDA® Granular
2 tbsp. rice vinegar
1 tbsp. sesame oil
¼ cup strong tea

In a food processor, puree all the ingredients to make an almost smooth sauce.

If you used chunky peanut butter, the sauce will be more textured but just as delicious.

Tarragon Mustard Sauce

Preparation Time: 2 minutes
Serving Size: 2 Tbsp
Serves: 9

1 jar Dijon Mustard (8 oz.)
2 tsp. dried tarragon leaves
1 tbsp. canola oil
1 tbsp. honey
2 tbsp. white wine
2 tsp. SPLENDA® Granular

Stove Top Heating

In small saucepan, combine all ingredients. Heat on low-medium heat stirring frequently until warm, approximately 5 minutes.

Microwave Heating

In small microwave-safe bowl, combine all ingredients. Microwave on high for 1-2 minutes, or until warm.

Hollandaise Sauce (easy)

3 Egg Yolks
   1 Tbsp. hot Water
   1 Tbsp. fresh Lime Juice
   Dash of Hot Sauce
   Salt and freshly ground Black Pepper to Taste
   ¼ tsp. Paprika
   ¼ cup fresh chopped

For the sauce: Place the yolks, water and lemon juice in a blender or food processor.
Blend on medium speed for one minute.
With the blender running, pour the hot, melted butter through the opening in the lid of the blender.
Season with hot sauce, salt and pepper.
Keep warm

Dark Chocolate Fudge Sauce

2 squares unsweetened chocolate, broken up

1/3 cup water

½ cup Splenda

3 tbsp butter, cut in small pieces

½ tsp vanilla

Put chocolate and water in a heavy medium saucepan.

Cook over low heat, stirring with a rubber spatula until chocolate has melted and blended with water, about 3 to 5 minutes.

Add sugar; continue cooking over low heat, stirring constantly, until sugar is dissolved, about 4 to 5 minutes.

Remove from heat and stir in butter until melted and blended.

Stir in vanilla and serve immediately.

Makes about 1 cup of chocolate sauce.

Peanut Butter Fudge Sauce

1 Dark Chocolate Sauce Recipe
1 cup creamy peanut butter
½ cup heavy cream

In a 2-quart microwavable bowl, place peanut butter, and cream.

Microwave on HIGH for 1 1/2 minutes, until boiling.

Add chocolate sauce and stir until combined.

Store in the refrigerator; warm up to serve over ice cream.

Makes 2 1/2 cups

The Salsa

2 green bell pepper, chopped
1 red or yellow bell pepper, chopped
Corn from two fresh ears, cut off cob (leave out corn until third phase)
3 ripe tomatoes chopped
1 large Vidalia or Spanish onion, chopped
1 large red onion, chopped
1 Jalapeno pepper, seeded and chopped
1/2 cup chopped fresh cilantro
juice of 3 fresh limes
3 Cubanelle peppers, seeded and chopped
1 tbsp chili garlic paste (from Oriental grocery store also called Sambal Olek)
5 cloves garlic chopped
2 tbsp Old Bay Seasoning

Place seeded Jalapeno and garlic in a mini food processor and chop until fine. This keeps you from finding a large piece of either in your mouth and spreads the flavors evenly through the salsa.

Hand chop all the remaining vegetables

Mix all ingredients well.

Best if allowed to stand 12 hours.

You can mix and match any other pepper varieties of your choice in this salsa.

Taco Soup

1lb ground turkey breast
1 can red beans
1 can black beans
1 can of Rotel tomatoes (tomato bits w/mild, medium, or
   hot chilies)
1 small can tomato sauce
1 large can tomato sauce with bits
1 can of cut green beans; drained
1 pack dry mix taco seasoning
1 pack dry mix Hidden Valley Ranch Original Salad
   Dressing
2 cans of water
1 beef bouillon cube

Spray a skillet with Pam and cook the ground turkey
breast; drain any left over liquid;

Add all the other ingredients in the order they appear; stir
well;

Bring to a boil; lower the heat and simmer for about 30
minutes; stir often and add more water if it gets too thick.

This can go in a thermos as a quick and delicious lunch.

Gazpacho

1 (10 1/2-ounce) can low sodium tomato soup, undiluted
1/3 cup finely chopped onion
2 tbsp red wine red wine vinegar
1¾ cup no-salt-added tomato juice
½ cup finely chopped green pepper
2/3 cup finely chopped cucumber
1 tbsp lemon juice
1 clove garlic, minced
½ cup chopped tomato
½ tsp pepper
¼ tsp salt
¼ tsp hot sauce

Thinly sliced cucumber (optional)
Fat Free Sour Cream (optional)

Combine tomato soup with next 12 ingredients in a
covered refrigerator container; stir well.

Cover and chill at least 8 hours.

To serve, ladle soup into individual bowls, and garnish
with cucumber slices and sour cream, if desired.

Yield: 5 cups

Summer Vegetable Soup

1 small onion, quartered and thinly sliced
1 tbsp olive or canola oil
4 cups reduced-sodium chicken broth
1 cup sliced zucchini
1 can (15-1/2 ounces) navy beans, rinsed and drained
½ cup cut fresh green beans (2-inch pieces)
½ cup chopped peeled tomato
¼ tsp pepper
1/8 tsp ground turmeric
¼ cup chopped celery leaves
2 tbsp tomato paste

In a large saucepan, sauté onion in oil until tender.

Add the next seven ingredients.

Bring to a boil.

Reduce heat; cover and simmer for 20-30 minutes or until vegetables are tender.

Stir in celery leaves and tomato paste.

Cover and let stand for 5 minutes before serving.

Yield: 4 servings.

Desserts

Snicker Doodles

Resembles snicker doodle cookies or spice cake...

1 15oz container ricotta
1 Tbsp Splenda
1 Tbsp Sugar-Free Vanilla Instant Pudding Powder
(optional)
1 tsp vanilla extract
1 Tbsp water or cream (more or less, depending on how
thick/creamy you like it)
1/2 tsp cinnamon
1/8 tsp nutmeg
Tiny pinch cloves

Place all ingredients in food processor.

Adjust the amount of spices to your liking before
mixing...you can always add more if you like.

Process well, till smooth and creamy.

Makes 4 servings

Baked Ricotta Cheesecake

1/2-2/3 cup of your favorite ricotta dessert flavor

(Already pre-mixed/flavored the way you like it),

1 egg (or 1/4 cup egg substitute),

Mix ricotta and egg and beat with a wire whip until well combined, pour into a sprayed custard cup, bake at 325 until done. (I usually check after 15-20 minutes)

Mock Key Lime Pie

1 cup of ricotta
½ pkg sugar-free lime gelatin (1½ tsp)

Put both ingredients in a bowl

Whip it with a hand-held Cuisinart or a mini food processor until it is thoroughly mixed and free of lumps.

Divide into 2 servings and top it with fat-free, no sugar whipped topping.

Try other flavors!

Blizzard

½ oz (2 T) sugar free, fat free any flavor Gelatin Brand
Instant Pudding Mix
1 cup skim milk
1 cup ice
2 Tbsp Whey Protein (optional)

In a blender mix the pudding mix powder and the milk.
After it is completely blended add the 1-cup of ice. Blend
until ice is thoroughly incorporated. Enjoy one HUGE
tasty treat!

Pumpkin Pie Minis

This is only for phase three because of the glycemic index of pumpkin.

1 15oz can 100% Pure Pumpkin
1-cup liquid egg substitute (4 eggs)
1½ cups Splenda
½ tsp cinnamon
¼ tsp ginger
tiny pinch cloves
(or use "pumpkin pie spice")
½ tsp salt

Preheat oven 350 degrees.

Blend ingredients together with a whisk.

Line a 12-section muffin pan with **foil** cups.

Spray the cups with cooking spray.

Divide mixture evenly among the muffin cups.

Bake at 350 degrees for 20 minutes, until a knife inserted comes out clean.

Refrigerate.

Serve with fat-free, sugar free whipped topping.

Unbaked Chocolate Peanut Butter Oatmeal Cookies
2nd and 3rd phase recipe

1 cup I Can't Believe Its Not Butter
2 cups Splenda
½ cup whipping cream
¾ cup chunky peanut butter (Only fresh from the Deli, no jars!)
3 cups oatmeal
6 tbsp powdered cocoa
1 tsp vanilla

Place the butter, sugar and cream in a saucepan and bring to a boil over high heat; stirring.

At first the Splenda will clump but just keep stirring, it will smooth out.

Boil one minute, stirring constantly. Remove from heat and add peanut butter, oatmeal and cocoa, then the vanilla.

Stir well and drop by rounded teaspoonfuls on waxed paper-lined cookie sheets. Refrigerate until set. Store in airtight container in refrigerator. Makes about 40.

Note: This is a second and third phase recipe. It is critical that you use the correct peanut butter. You want fresh ground from the deli, as it is pure peanuts and nothing else. You can also make peanut butter at home in your food processor with dry roasted peanuts and a little safflower oil. All peanut butter sold in jars is loaded with carbs in the form of sugar.

Oatmeal... use only the Old-fashioned real oatmeal. No Quick, no instant. This ensures that you get the whole grain, not the stuff where the good fiber has been milled away so that it cooks quicker.

Low Carb Gelatin Cream Cheese Pie

If you want a crust you could easily make one using ground pecans or almonds, a little butter and Splenda.

Press into bottom of pie pan and bake at 350°F for about 5-6 minutes.

Then add the Gelatin filling after crust has cooled.

2 small boxes sugar-free Gelatin, any flavor
3 oz. cream cheese, softened
4 tbsp. heavy cream
2 c. boiling water

Pour water over both boxes of sugar-free Gelatin.

Stir to dissolve.

Add cream cheese.

Beat with a mixer until the cheese is completely mixed in. It will be "frothy."

Stir in 2 cups cold water.

Whip 4 tbsp. of heavy cream until stiff.

Lightly whisk the whipped cream into the Gelatin mixture.

Cover and refrigerate until firm.

It will separate into 3 layers. Clear Gelatin on the bottom. A flavored cream cheese layer in the middle. A flavored whipped cream layer on top.

Servings: 4 Carbs 1 per serving

Fast Gelatin Treat

Ingredients:
1-Large Box of Sugar Free Gelatin, any flavor
8 oz.-Cream Cheese
Boil 2 cups of water

Dissolve Gelatin in boiling water.

Soften cream cheese in microwave and stir until smooth
and creamy.

Slowly add gelatin to cream cheese mixture and continue
stirring until well blended.

Add 2 cups of cold water, mix well and chill until firm.

Serve and enjoy.

It's delicious and low carb! How can you beat that?

Low Carb Crustless Pumpkin Cheesecake

2 pkg gelatin (Knox)
1 cup boiling water
16 oz cream cheese at room temp
1 tsp vanilla
½ cup Splenda
½ cup canned unsweetened pumpkin
½ tsp cinnamon
dash of ground cloves
dash of nutmeg

Dissolve gelatin in boiling water in a mixing bowl.

Stir well

Cut the cream cheese into small pieces and add to the gelatin

Beat with mixer until well blended

Add vanilla, pumpkin, Splenda and spice

Beat well

Pour into 9" pie plate and chill for several hours

Cut into 8 slices

Chocolate-Almond Crisps

2/3 cup unsweetened cocoa powder
½ cup ground almonds
½ tsp ground cinnamon
1/8 tsp ground nutmeg
1/8 tsp salt
4 egg whites
¼ tsp almond extract
2 cups sugar substitute

Preheat oven to 250 F. Line 2 baking sheets with parchment paper

In a medium bowl, combine cocoa, almonds, cinnamon, nutmeg, and salt. Mix well and set aside.

In a large bowl, using an electric mixer set on high speed, beat egg whites and almond extract until foamy. Gradually add sugar, beating until stiff, but not dry, peaks form. Add cocoa mixture, beating until blended.

Drop batter by rounded tablespoonfuls, 2 inches apart, on prepared baking sheets. Using the back of a spoon, smooth cookies into 3-inch rounds.

Bake cookies until firm, about 30 minutes. Turn off oven and cool cookies inside the oven until dry and crisp, about 1 hour.

Makes 1 dozen cookies

Cream Cheese "Truffles"

2 oz of low fat cream cheese with
3 Tbsp of Splenda and
1 Tbsp of unsweetened cocoa.
Additional cocoa and Splenda for rolling

Mix all ingredients together

Roll into small balls

Roll in a cocoa/Splenda mixture.

Store in Refrigerator.

You can vary this recipe by adding
1 Tbsp peanut butter to the cream cheese.

Homemade Ice Cream

Important Note

All the homemade recipes are just wonderful right out of
the ice cream machine. ½ cup is the serving amount. You
will have leftover product, which should be put in a plastic
container and stored, in the freezer. Homemade Ice Cream
will then freeze very hard and must be tempered 30
minutes in the refrigerator before serving. Return unused
portion to the freezer and then re-temper before serving
again. Ice cream must always be stored covered in an
airtight container, as it will easily pick up other flavors
from your refrigerator or freezer.

Butter Pecan Ice Cream Recipe

16 oz (500ml) single/light cream
16 oz (500ml) heavy/double cream,
½ cup Sugar Twin brown sugar
2 tbsp butter
½ cup of pecan nuts (chopped), toasted first if you like
1 tsp vanilla extract

Place the single cream, sugar and butter into a saucepan and mix together over a low heat. Stir until the mixture starts to bubble around the edges. Remove the saucepan from the heat and allow to cool. When the mixture is cold transfer it to an ice cream maker and stir in the double cream and vanilla extract. Freeze according to the manufacturer's instructions but remember to add the pecans as the ice cream starts to harden

Vanilla Ice Cream Recipe (Custard Base)

4 egg yolks
½ pint (250ml) milk

½ pint (250ml) double/heavy cream
½ cup Splenda
1 Vanilla Bean

Slice open the vanilla bean and scrape all the seeds into the milk in a heavy saucepan.

Put the rest of the vanilla bean in the milk as well.

Scald the milk (bring slowly up to boiling point but do not allow it to boil. Do this on low heat).

Separately, beat together the egg yolks and Splenda until thick.

Stir about ¼ cup of the hot mixture into the egg mixture while stirring rapidly.

Then whisk the egg mixture into the hot mixture while whisking rapidly.

Heat gently, stirring until the custard thickens (DO NOT BRING TO A BOIL as it will curdle. If that happens you can place the whole thing in the blender or food processor to attempt to smooth it out)

When you can see a film form over the back of your spoon it's time to remove the saucepan from the heat. Leave to cool. When cool remove the vanilla bean.

This custard base can be used in many other recipes.

When the custard base is cold, stir in the cream, then transfer the whole mixture into an ice cream maker and freeze according to the manufacturer's instructions.

Quick Vanilla Ice Cream

½ pint (250ml) single/light cream
1 small can of sugar free condensed milk
1-2 tsp vanilla extract (according to taste)

Pour all ingredients into a mixing bowl and mix until smooth.

Transfer the whole mixture into an ice cream maker and freeze according to the manufacturer's directions.

Crunchy Pecan Maple Ice Cream

4 oz (100g) pecans chopped
2 oz (50g) butter
2 tbsp brown sugar Sugar-Twin
2 tbsp sugar free maple syrup
12 oz (375ml) milk
12 oz (375ml) double/heavy cream

Using a frying pan, slowly melt the butter then add the chopped pecans.

Sprinkle on the brown sugar, stir and cook on a medium heat for approx 3-4 minutes until the nuts are crisp Watch the pecans carefully as over cooking them will result in a bitter taste.

Remove from the pan and place to one side to cool. In a separate mixing bowl, pour in the milk, stir in the cream and then add the fried, chopped pecan nuts.

Still stirring add the maple syrup until blended in.

Transfer the complete mixture into an ice cream maker and follow the manufacturer's instructions.

Chocolate Ice Cream

5 egg yolks,
16 oz (500ml) milk,
8 oz (250ml) double/heavy cream,
½ cup Splenda,
3 tbsp of cocoa powder

Create a custard base (see instructions from the vanilla ice cream recipe) using eggs, milk, and Splenda.

Upon removing the saucepan from the heat to allow the mixture to cool, add the cocoa.

Chill the custard until it's really cold.

Once chilled, mix until slushy.

Add the heavy cream and mix well.

Transfer the mixture to an ice cream maker and freeze according to the manufacturer's instructions.

Variation: Add 2 TBSP Peanut Butter to the mixture with the cocoa and stir to blend well.

Closing Thoughts

Eating out on a low carb plan is not only possible, it's enjoyable! Just leave the potatoes and rice in the kitchen! Here are a couple of tips that come from my experience.

I don't go to a restaurant hungry. I eat a stick of string cheese, on my way if need be!

At first it was hard to ask to have the bread removed from the table, but gradually I realized how awful I had felt from all the excess carbs and I really began to notice the difference in my energy level, and then bread didn't appeal to me and removing it became second nature!

A trick I learned from my daughter… when you are served a salad with dressing on the side in a restaurant, place the dressing dish on the table and barely dip the tines of your fork in the salad dressing before spearing a bite. Remember, I said barely!

Fast Food… I've looked at all the nutritional charts from the popular fast food restaurants and I can tell you that there is absolutely nothing that fits the plan unless you are very careful.

If you simply have no choice then stick with the salads, minus croutons (come on, they're awful anyway!), minus Chinese noodles (a different way to fry flour!) and minus at least three quarters of even the low fat dressings. Open the dressing package and use tiny drops on your salad. Throw the rest away… yes I know there are starving children somewhere, but putting that dressing directly on your hips isn't feeding them either!

One of my clients was just sure she could never stick with the plan because, social butterfly that she is, all the obligatory cocktail parties would do her in. As a hypnotist I explained to her that contrary to popular belief, I could not twitch my nose and cause the weight to drop off, she was going to have to do the work herself. Here is her plan…

Before a public function she has a small meal, not just a snack. This small meal is made up mostly of protein. At the event itself she first orders mineral water with lime, then, if she wants another drink she has a glass of red wine. If she still feels the need to have another drink then it's another mineral water with lime, etc. See how this works?

How about a private cocktail party? Even easier… make a plate of something you know you can eat and present it to the hostess. What hostess will turn down an extra appetizer? Eat what you brought. Still, you shouldn't attend any event hungry. Never. At all events stick to red wine and only two glasses.

Let's talk about cheating. Are you going to? Sure. You're human aren't you? Just say to yourself that next meal you'll get right back on the plan. Remember that this plan is for life and deprivation just won't get it.

Here is an analogy given to me by the renowned hypnotist, Don Mottin, "If you back your car out of the garage and crunch up the back bumper, would you immediately put the car in drive and crunch up the front bumper?" Of course not. So don't let me hear you say, "I had a _____ and so now I've quit the plan." Cheat. Get over it. Move on.

On hypnosis and weight reduction... I did it and so can you. Hypnosis, as the series on Dateline made clear, really does work. Let me tell you a little bit about the "why".

Here is the explanation from a hypnotist's point of view. When the conscious mind is in agreement with the subconscious then the task is completed. Let there be just a small amount of disagreement between them and whatever the task, it never stands a chance of success.

So sometimes, no matter how much the conscious wants to be thin, the subconscious has other ideas. Excess weight is not seen as a negative by the subconscious, quite the contrary, the subconscious has added the weight for its own very good reasons and will only release it when the reason to hold it has been alleviated.

I'd like to share a secret with you... one that came to me only after several months on a low carb food plan. You see one day I had the big AH HA... I had solved the problem... the fear of getting fat again was gone. My sense of relief made me weak, and in the next breath, made me stronger than I have ever been. What a rush! Now I can look at a plate of cookies and realize that I like cookies, no, I love cookies, but I like my slim, trim body better than I ever liked cookies. You can get there, too. Finally, you can have the body of your dreams.

You can do it...I know you can. Why not start today?

What have you got to lose?

Notes

Contents

3

Preface

Biography Today is a magazine designed and written for the young reader—ages 9 and above—and covers individuals that librarians and teachers tell us that young people want to know about most: entertainers, athletes, writers, illustrators, cartoonists, and political leaders.

The Plan of the Work

The publication was especially created to appeal to young readers in a format they can enjoy reading and readily understand. Each issue contains approximately 10 sketches arranged alphabetically. Each entry provides at least one picture of the individual profiled, and bold-faced rubrics lead the reader to information on birth, youth, early memories, education, first jobs, marriage and family, career highlights, memorable experiences, hobbies, and honors and awards. Each of the entries ends with a list of easily accessible sources designed to lead the student to further reading on the individual and a current address. Retrospetive entries are also included, written to provide a perspective on the individual's entire career. These restrospective entries are clearly marked in both the table of contents and at the beginning of the entry.

Biographies are prepared by Omnigraphics editors after extensive research, utilizing the most current materials available. Those sources that are generally available to students appear in the list of further reading at the end of the sketch.

Indexes

Cumulative indexes are an important component of *Biography Today*. Each issue of the *Biography Today* General Series includes a Cumulative Names Index, which comprises all individuals profiled in *Biography Today* since the series began in 1992. In addition, we compile three other indexes: the Cumulative General Index, Places of Birth Index, and Birthday Index. These three indexes are featured on our web site, www.biographytoday.com. All *Biography Today* indexes are cumulative, including all individuals profiled in both the General Series and the Subject Series.

Our Advisors

This series was reviewed by an Advisory Board comprised of librarians, children's literature specialists, and reading instructors to ensure that the concept of this publication—to provide a readable and accessible biographical magazine for young readers—was on target. They evaluated the title as it developed, and their suggestions have proved invaluable. Any errors, however, are ours alone. We'd like to list the Advisory Board members, and to thank them for their efforts.

Our Advisory Board stressed to us that we should not shy away from controversial or unconventional people in our profiles, and we have tried to follow their advice. The Advisory Board also mentioned that the sketches might be useful in reluctant reader and adult literacy programs, and we would value any comments librarians might have about the suitability of our magazine for those purposes.

Your Comments Are Welcome

Our goal is to be accurate and up-to-date, to give young readers information they can learn from and enjoy. Now we want to know what you think. Take a look at this issue of *Biography Today*, on approval. Write or call me with your comments. We want to provide an excellent source of biographical information for young people. Let us know how you think we're doing.

Cherie Abbey
Managing Editor, *Biography Today*
Omnigraphics, Inc.
615 Griswold Street
Detroit, MI 48226

editor@biographytoday.com
www.biographytoday.com

Congratulations!

Congratulations to the following individuals and libraries, who are receiving a free copy of *Biography Today*, Vol. 14, No. 1 for suggesting people who appear in this issue:

Anne Heidemann, Youth Services Coordinator Librarian, Chippewa River District Library System, Mt. Pleasant, MI

Miranda Louis, Cambridge, MA

Joy Wald, Hobart Middle School, Hobart, OK

Joanna Wong, San Francisco, CA

Jack Black 1969-
American Actor and Musician
Star of *Shallow Hal* and *School of Rock,* Member of the
Spoof Rock Duo *Tenacious D*

BIRTH

Jack Black was born Thomas Black on April 7, 1969, in Santa
Monica, California, although his birthplace has also been list-
ed as Edmonton, Alberta, Canada. He is the only child of Tom
and Judy Black, both of whom are satellite communications
engineers. Because his parents had both been married previ-
ously and divorced when he was still in grade school, he has
several half-siblings.

YOUTH

"Jack was my nickname and it just stuck," Black explains. He is reluctant to divulge much about his childhood, although he describes it as "hip and confusing." He was raised in Hermosa Beach, California, by parents who fought constantly and divorced when he was ten. His father left the country and started a new family, and Jack was raised by his Jewish mother. Although he describes both his parents as "loving," he felt like he never got enough attention from them and spent the rest of his life trying to compensate.

"I remember Hebrew school, which I had to go to three times a week," Black says. "We'd have recess when we weren't studying. We'd be playing around, and I remember getting some candy and putting it in the bathroom and then going outside and saying, 'There's a magic dragon in the bathroom.' And a couple of kids would run in there, and I'd turn off the lights and make dragon sounds and turn on the lights and say, 'Man, the dragon left some candy.' It was to try and make them believe in magic and stuff. I really liked being the source of entertainment."

Black's interest in rock music also dates back to his childhood. "I was really into [the rock band] Journey when I was a kid," he recalls. "I went to the record store one day to get their new album, and this older kid was like, 'Oh man, you don't want to get that — get this.' He handed me Ozzy Osbourne's *Blizzard of Ozz*. It changed my world, and I became a heavy metal-er."

> "I was really into [the rock band] Journey when I was a kid," Black recalls. "I went to the record store one day to get their new album, and this older kid was like, 'Oh man, you don't want to get that — get this.' He handed me Ozzy Osbourne's **Blizzard of Ozz**. It changed my world, and I became a heavy metal-er."

EDUCATION

Black was never a very good student and spent a lot of time pretending to be sick so he wouldn't have to go to school. He was kicked out of Culver City Junior High School for using drugs, after which he was sent to a Los Angeles school for troubled teens called the Poseidon School. It was here that Black first became interested in acting, appearing in his first commercial—for Atari, a pioneer in the computer and video games industry—at the age of 13. "I knew that if my friends saw me on TV, it would be the answer to all my prayers," he explains. "Because then they would have to worship me and everyone would know I was awesome. And I was awesome—for three days. Then it wore off. But it gave me the hunger."

After a year at Poseidon, Black went to Crossroads School, a private high school in Santa Monica with a strong performing arts program. At Crossroads he was the class clown, but he also got involved in school plays and started thinking about becoming a rock musician. "I performed in a band," he says. "We went and played at a high school party, and we were doing a real earnest serious version of [the Black Sabbath song] 'Iron Man.' No one paid attention, everyone was talking to each other, and we couldn't even hear ourselves play. . . . We stopped in the middle of the song, didn't even finish, and said, 'Let's just leave. This sucks.'" It wasn't until several years later that Black discovered he could make a career for himself in rock music by playing songs that were deliberately bad.

After graduating from Crossroads in 1987, Black attended the University of California at Los Angeles (UCLA), where he majored in theater. "I did some stuff in there that I was proud of. I had some good plays," he says of his UCLA days, but basically "I was an awful student. I slept through everything." He dropped out of college at the end of his second year.

CAREER HIGHLIGHTS

The Actors' Gang

Soon after leaving UCLA, Black joined the Actors' Gang, a Los Angeles-based theater company founded by actor and director Tim Robbins. He spent several years acting in the group's productions, which included classic dramas like *Peer Gynt* by Henrik Ibsen and a play called *Carnage,* written by Robbins and performed at the Edinburgh Theater Festival in Scotland. Black got his first movie role as a groupie in *Bob Roberts,* Robbins's 1992 satire about a right-wing politician. After that, Black had small parts in a string of not-very-successful films in the early to mid-1990s, including *Demolition Man, The Neverending Story III,* and *Waterworld.* He also appeared on a number of television shows during that time, including episodes of "Picket Fences," "Touched by an Angel," and "The X-Files."

While Black was performing with the Actors' Gang in 1994 he met Kyle Gass, who shared his interest in rock music. Together they formed a heavy metal acoustic rock duo called Tenacious D, which they named after a basketball term used by sportscaster Marv Albert to describe tough defensive action. Tenacious D played songs and performed skits that poked fun at the egotism, anger, and posturing of many rock stars. Soon, the duo began to attract attention with their appearances at Los Angeles clubs. Both men were overweight and Gass was balding, but this didn't stop them from strutting across the stage as if they were celebrity rockers. The *Los Angeles Times* called them "a mix of the Smothers Brothers, Cheech and Chong, Beavis and Butthead, and Spinal Tap."

In 1995 Black appeared in the Academy Award-nominated film *Dead Man Walking,* directed by Tim Robbins, which starred Sean Penn as a convicted criminal facing execution and Susan Sarandon as the nun who tries to help him. Black's performance as Penn's brother led to supporting roles in more films. In 1996 he appeared in *The Cable Guy,* which was directed by Ben Stiller and also starred Jim Carrey and Matthew Broderick. Black played Broderick's best friend, who suggests bribing the cable TV installer to get more channels. The movie didn't do very well at the box office, nor did any of the other movies in which Black appeared in the late 1990s, including the science fiction parody *Mars Attacks!,* a Bruce Willis thriller called *The Jackal,* and *Enemy of the State,* which starred Will Smith. In 1998 Black had a supporting role in *Johnny Skidmarks,* a thriller about a crime scene photographer starring Peter Gallagher and Frances McDormand, in which Black played Gallagher's former brother-in-law. While *Variety* found the movie "gloomy" and "not very convincing," it singled out Black's performance as noteworthy. The following year, Black played a would-be ventriloquist in another film directed by Tim Robbins, *Cradle Will Rock.*

> *Actor John Cusack commented that Jack Black "is great because . . . he's the king of somewhere. It might not be Earth, but it's definitely somewhere."*

The Rise of Tenacious D

While Black's acting career progressed slowly throughout the 1990s, he began to develop a cult following as part of Tenacious D. He and Gass started appearing in 10-minute spots following episodes of "Mr. Show with Bob and David," a comedy sketch series on HBO. They performed what *Entertainment Weekly* called "really terrific 'bad' songs," characterized by deliberately meaningless lyrics like, "It was a big day on Jesus Ranch/I fell in love with a baked potato." By 1999 they had their own series on HBO in which

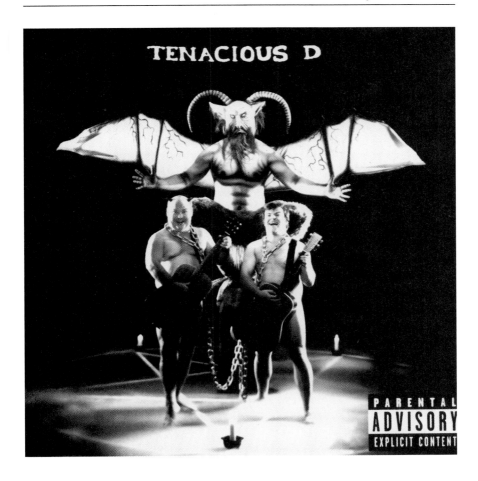

they competed with each other for the attentions of a punk record store clerk named Flama. They also continued to parody the behavior of rock stars with songs that a critic from the Colorado Springs *Gazette* described as "the musical equivalent of gourmet marshmallows."

In 2001 Gass and Black released their first CD, called *Tenacious D*. It entered the *Billboard* chart at No. 33 and almost went platinum, selling far more copies than anyone had anticipated. The album had songs and skits with titles like "Kielbasa," "Karate Schnitzel," and "Sasquatch," and the pair's combination of heavy metal music and bathroom humor had an underground appeal that threatened to attract a mainstream audience. Actor John Cusack, another former Actors' Gang member and one of the duo's greatest fans, commented that Black "is great because . . . he's the king of somewhere. It might not be Earth, but it's definitely somewhere."

John Cusack, Jack Black, Todd Louiso, and Tim Robbins in the record store in a scene from High Fidelity.

High Fidelity

It was John Cusack who gave Black his first major movie role in *High Fidelity,* a film that Cusack himself starred in. In fact, Cusack also co-wrote the screenplay, which was based on the novel of the same name by Nick Hornby. Cusack's character, Rob Gordon, runs a record store, where he employs Barry (played by Black). A snobby music lover, Barry knows everything there is to know about vintage vinyl recordings and routinely insults customers who come in to buy mainstream music. As Owen Gleiberman wrote in *Entertainment Weekly,* "He plays Barry as an amusingly wired, passive-aggressive bully who holds the entire universe of popular music within his brain, all of it meticulously catalogued into the good, the bad, or the sublime. If you disagree with him, you're one of the unenlightened, and he can barely bring himself to speak to you."

Rob has recently been dumped by his girlfriend, and he spends most of his time hanging around the store making up "top five" lists of songs with Barry and another employee named Dick. The list-making leads to flashbacks about Rob's failed relationships with women. Barry, who dreams of being a musician himself some day, finally gets a chance to show off his talents as the movie draws to a close.

His performance as Barry was a breakout role for Black and led critics to compare him to John Belushi, the former "Saturday Night Live" comedian and star of the movie *Animal House*. Like Belushi, Black had a chubby physique, elastic face, and very expressive eyebrows. His "explosively bizarre" form of comedy reminded many people of Belushi as well. The *New York Daily News* commented that "When director Stephen Frears worked with this guy, he must have yelled, 'Let 'er rip!' instead of 'Action!'" *High Fidelity,* which was released in 2000, received favorable reviews, became a big audience favorite, and established Black as a comic actor.

Moving Up to Leading Roles

In 2001, Black appeared in a teen comedy called *Saving Silverman.* Black, Jason Biggs, and Steve Zahn play best friends who belong to a band that has modeled itself after Neil Diamond. They perform in long-haired wigs, wear tight black pants and flashy shirts, and call themselves Diamonds in the Rough. But when a beautiful psychologist (Amanda Peet) develops a romantic interest in Silverman (Biggs), she decides that he should stop seeing his friends. Desperate to save him — and their friendships — Black and Zahn take drastic steps. They kidnap Peet and try to reunite Silverman with his high school sweetheart, who is now training to become a nun. Teen audiences enjoyed the film, but it was a flop with movie critics — for example, the *Los Angeles Times* called it "a standard issue numbskull comedy" and "disposable as a paper towel." But Black and Zahn were singled out by the critics for their performances. "They're great together," a critic for the *Washington Post* said, "even in a bottom-of-the-barrel comedy like this."

> *"He plays Barry as an amusingly wired, passive-aggressive bully who holds the entire universe of popular music within his brain, all of it meticulously catalogued into the good, the bad, or the sublime. If you disagree with him, you're one of the unenlightened, and he can barely bring himself to speak to you."*
> — Owen Gleiberman, **Entertainment Weekly**

Black got a chance to play his first leading role in 2001. *Shallow Hal* is a romantic comedy about Hal Larson (Black), a less-than-perfect-looking man who has a very inflated view of his appeal to women. He only pursues gorgeous women, even though he is repeatedly rejected by them. He gets caught in an elevator one day with Tony Robbins, a self-help guru, who

Scenes from Saving Silverman *(top),* Shallow Hal *(center), and* Orange County *(bottom).*

hypnotizes him so that from now on, he only sees women's inner beauty. Larson immediately falls in love with Rosemary, a Peace Corps volunteer who he sees as slim and beautiful but who is really very overweight. Rosemary is played by Gwyneth Paltrow, who wears an inflated "fat suit" in many scenes. Directed by the Farrelly brothers, who also directed *Dumb and Dumber* and *There's Something about Mary*, the film provoked mixed reactions from critics. Much of the film's humor was based on "fat jokes" about Rosemary, which many critics and viewers found offensive. But almost all praised Black's performance as Hal. Roger Ebert, writing for the *Chicago Sun-Times*, found the movie "very funny, but . . . also surprisingly moving at times," especially in its portrayal of characters who are struggling to overcome the labels imposed on them by others. Ebert observed that Black "struts through with the blissful confidence of a man who knows he was born for stardom, even though he doesn't look like your typical Gwyneth Paltrow boyfriend."

In 2002 Black appeared in the suburban teen comedy *Orange County* as Lance, the deadbeat older brother of a high school over-achiever named Shaun (Colin Hanks). Shaun is desperate to get into Stanford University so that he can study with his literary hero, Marcus Skinner (Kevin Kline). But when Shaun is rejected because his school records have gotten mixed up, Lance tries to intervene and ends up burning down the admissions building. In addition to Kline, the impressive supporting cast included John Lithgow, Catherine O'Hara, Harold Ramis, Ben Stiller, and Lily Tomlin. Once again, Black's ability to portray inspired nuttiness triggered comparisons with the late John Belushi and won positive comments in the midst of otherwise lukewarm reviews. Still, the movie proved to be a big hit with teen viewers.

School of Rock

Black finally got a chance to play the kind of role he had dreamed of in the 2003 hit movie, *School of Rock*. He plays Dewey Finn, a failed rock musician who gets hired as a substitute teacher at a snobby prep school by impersonating his roommate. Dewey takes rock music — and himself — very seriously, sharing such bits of wisdom as "I serve society by rocking" and "For those about to rock, we salute you." In the classroom, he dispenses with his fifth graders' normal studies and concentrates instead on teaching them the only thing he really understands: rock music. They form their own rock band, and Dewey teaches them what songs to play, how to move, and what kind of faces to make as they prepare for a "battle of the bands" at the movie's end. Meanwhile, he must confront the school's uptight headmistress, played by Joan Cusack, who turns out to be a closet rock music fan herself.

The script was based on the true story of *The Langley Schools Music Project*, an album recorded in the late 1970s by a teacher in rural Canada who taught his students to perform rock and pop classics like "Good Vibrations," "Mandy," "Space Oddity," and "Desperado." The result was a cult hit album that, according to *School of Rock* script writer Mike White, "had both a comic aspect and a sweetness." White created the character of Dewey Finn expressly for Black, whom he knew from working on *Orange County*. "Dude, I was born to play this part," Black says. "Everything about it lines up perfectly with my strengths. Which include rocking. Which also include being superintense and passionate about stuff."

> "*Let's come right out and say it:* **School of Rock** *made me laugh harder than any movie I've seen this year. . . . It's a bravura, all-stops-out, inexhaustibly inventive performance. I don't know how much was improvised, and how much comes from White's sharp screenplay, but Black may never again get and part that displays his mad-dog comic ferocity to such brilliant effect.*"
> — *David Ansen,* **Newsweek**

Praise for Black's performance was unanimous. Viewers loved it, as the film appealed to parents as well as their children; Black himself admitted that "kids respond to my high-energy kind of ridiculousness." And movie reviewers were equally enthusiastic. As the critic Owen Gleiberman wrote for *Entertainment Weekly*, "[In *School of Rock*, Black] reaches deep inside his riffing, strutting, head-banging self to give the most joyful performance I've seen all year. Black is still a happy geek in perpetual overdrive, only now he draws on his musical skill, and his hipster shamelessness, to deliver the acting equivalent of a perfect power chord crunched with a demon smile." Those accolades were echoed by David Ansen in *Newsweek*: "Let's come right out and say it: *School of Rock* made me laugh harder than any movie I've seen this year. The giggles start coming right at the get-go, when Jack Black, as the fiercely committed but less than inspired rock-and-roller Dewey Finn, howls his way through a song, then hurls himself shirtless and triumphant into the mosh pit . . . where the horrified crowd declines to catch him. . . . It's a bravura, all-stops-out, inexhaustibly inventive performance. I don't know how much

was improvised, and how much comes from White's sharp screenplay, but Black may never again get a part that displays his mad-dog comic ferocity to such brilliant effect."

Recent Projects and What Lies Ahead

Black's most recent movie project is the 2004 comedy *Envy*. Black plays Nick Vanderpart, a former factory worker who invented Vapoorize, a spray that makes dog poop evaporate. Now wealthy beyond belief, he is still de-

19

Black as Nick Vanderpart in the 2004 comedy Envy.

voted to his former co-worker and best friend, Tim Dingman, played by Ben Stiller. Tim had turned down the chance to invest just $2,000 in Vapoorize, thereby missing out on becoming rich himself. Now, he's sick with envy over his friend's success, which drives him to make some terrible choices. Despite the comic cast, the movie never really lived up to expectations, and it received generally lukewarm reviews.

Black claims that his first passion is still music. In late 2003 he released a DVD collection called *Tenacious D: The Complete Masterworks, Volume One*. It combines concert footage of Black and Gass with some of the short sketches they originally performed on HBO. Black hopes that the DVD will pave the way for a feature film that he has co-written with Liam Lynch about Tenacious D's "rise to power" from playing in obscure coffee houses to performing in front of huge concert audiences. "The weird thing is, nobody that's read it likes it so far," Black confesses. But he confidently predicts that the film will be "not just the best movie ever, but one of the great things ever. Like the pyramids."

Despite his recent successes and the over-inflated self-confidence of his on-screen persona, Black remains insecure about his talents. "I stress over career decisions and what people think of me," he says. "I'm always scared, thinking I'm going to be bad in everything." At the same time, the characters that he plays are usually "swaggering and cocksure, utterly convinced of their own studliness even when dressed in just a pair of sagging briefs," according to the *New York Times*. "To the rest of the world, these characters may look like losers and meatheads, but Black never mocks their delusions of grandeur, playing them instead with the sincere affection of a man who has himself spent hours playing air guitar in front of the mirror."

MARRIAGE AND FAMILY

Black has lived in the Hollywood Hills for several years with his girlfriend, Laura Kightlinger, whom he describes as "funnier than me." Kightlinger is an actress, a stand-up comedian, and a writer for the television series "Will and Grace." Black says that living with another comedian can be stressful. "When we're both working, we fight a lot. We both want the other one to be our personal assistant, and neither of us is willing to do it."

Will Black and Kightlinger get married and have a family some day? He doesn't see it happening. "I'm kind of a kid [myself]," he explains. "I'd have to do some growing up that I don't really want to do." Black also admits that his parents' failed marriage made a lasting impression on him.

MAJOR INFLUENCES

As a musician, Black has been influenced by what he calls "the school of heavy metal" — bands like Black Sabbath, Led Zeppelin, and AC/DC. He also likes Radiohead, the Foo Fighters, and Queens of the Stone Age. It was his mother who introduced him to heavy metal music, although she didn't do so deliberately. She went through a period where she was "trying different things and searching spiritually," Black recalls. "And there was this 'Jews for Jesus' phase where she gave me this tape that was some preacher saying rock is evil and here are some examples of music that would send you to hell." Although it wasn't what his mother intended,

> *Black's characters are usually "swaggering and cocksure, utterly convinced of their own studliness even when dressed in just a pair of sagging briefs," according to the* **New York Times.** *"To the rest of the world, these characters may look like losers and meatheads, but Black never mocks their delusions of grandeur, playing them instead with the sincere affection of a man who has himself spent hours playing air guitar in front of the mirror."*

21

Black says that the tape "exposed me to great heavy metal I hadn't heard before."

HOBBIES AND OTHER INTERESTS

Black describes himself as a "total shut-in" who rarely goes out to parties and would rather stay up all night and play Scrabble on the Internet. "When I'm relaxing," he says, "I just like to go to the movies, read a good book, or play video games."

SELECTED CREDITS

Films

Bob Roberts, 1992
Demolition Man, 1993
Airborne, 1993
Blind Justice, 1994
The Neverending Story III, 1994
Escape from Fantasia, 1994
Bye Bye, Love, 1995
Waterworld, 1995
Dead Man Walking, 1995
Bio-Dome, 1996
The Cable Guy, 1996
The Fan, 1996
Mars Attacks!, 1996
Crossworlds, 1996
The Jackal, 1997
Bongwater, 1998
Johnny Skidmarks, 1998
I Still Know What You Did Last Summer, 1998
Enemy of the State, 1998
Cradle Will Rock, 1999
Jesus' Son, 1999
High Fidelity, 2000
Saving Silverman, 2001
Shallow Hal, 2001
Orange County, 2002
Run Ronnie Run, 2002
School of Rock, 2003
Envy, 2004

Recordings

Tenacious D, 2001 (CD)
Tenacious D: The Complete Masterworks, Volume One, 2003 (DVD)

FURTHER READING

Books

Contemporary Theatre, Film, and Television, Vol. 32, 2000

Periodicals

Current Biography Yearbook, 2002
Entertainment Weekly, Nov. 16, 2001, p.102; Oct. 17, 2003, p.26
GQ, Oct. 2003, p.160
Los Angeles Daily News, Oct. 3, 2003, p.U6
Los Angeles Times, Apr. 1, 2000, p.F1
New York Times Magazine, Sep. 28, 2003, p.36
Newsweek, Sep. 29, 2003, p.52
Nickelodeon, Oct. 2004, p.78
People, Oct. 13, 2003, p.75
Premiere, Nov. 2001, p.28
Teen People, Nov. 1, 2003, p.62
Time, Oct. 6, 2003, p.73
Times (London), Jan. 24, 2004, magazine section, p.28
USA Today, Sep. 28, 2003, p.D1

Online Databases

Biography Resources Center Online, 2004, articles from *Contemporary Authors Online,* 2003; *Contemporary Theatre, Film, and Television,* 2000; and *Newsmakers,* 2002

ADDRESS

Jack Black
United Talent Agency
9560 Wilshire Blvd., 5th Floor
Los Angeles, CA 90212

WORLD WIDE WEB SITES

http://www.schoolofrockmovie.com
http://www.tenaciousd.com

Eve 1979-

American Rap Artist and Actress
Star of the Hit TV Show "Eve"

BIRTH

Eve was born Eve Jihan Jeffers in Philadelphia, Pennsylvania,
on November 10, 1979. Her mother, Julie Wilch, was a former
model who worked for a medical publishing company. Her
parents were never married, but Eve saw her father occasionally until she was 12. She and her mom lived in the Mill Creek
housing projects in Philadelphia with extended family when
Eve was young. They later moved to Germantown when her

mother married fashion designer Ron Wilch and gave birth to Eve's younger brother, Farrod.

YOUTH

Growing up, Eve says she was a tomboy. "I do have girlfriends, but I've always hung around with a lot of guys ever since I was little. I always wrestled and climbed trees and did boy stuff. I was a tomboy, but I was very aware that I was a girl. I love being feminine." Although she liked to play outside, she also loved to shop and put together new outfits. She credits her mother with helping her develop her sense of style. When she was growing up, her mother and aunt would take her shopping on Saturdays at Strawbridge's in Center City. "I had my own style. I never wanted to look like the group, the pack of girls who just walk around. They all looked alike and that just annoyed me. I wanted to be fly, but I wanted my own identity." Eve says her family was never poor, just broke all the time. "I don't want to be broke again, ever," she emphasizes.

"I had my own style. I never wanted to look like the group, the pack of girls who just walk around. They all looked alike and that just annoyed me. I wanted to be fly, but I wanted my own identity."

While she was growing up, Eve wasn't star-struck. She only had one poster on her wall, and it was of Michael Jordan. She didn't go to many concerts, either. "I didn't like concerts, because I felt like I needed to be onstage. . . . When I was young, I was like, 'I'm not going to nobody's concert. If I'm not performing, I don't want to go.'" Eve liked to sing when she was young, but when she was 13 she switched from singing to rap. That brought her a lot of attention, because at that point most rappers were male. She took the name Eve of Destruction and went to talent shows around Philadelphia. She performed with a group of girlfriends named D.G.P., for Dope Girl Posse; she also performed with her friend, Jennifer Pardue, as the group EDJP (Egypt), which stood for Eve of Destruction Jenny-Poo. They patterned their music after their musical role models: Mary J. Blige, Lauryn Hill, Queen Latifah, and MC Lite.

EDUCATION

Eve attended Martin Luther King Jr. High School in Philadelphia. She wasn't very involved in her schoolwork. "I got punished a lot," she admits.

"I got in trouble for cutting school, staying out late, lying about detention, and lying about homework. I hated high school. I always knew there was something else." Instead of doing her schoolwork, she was putting a lot of energy into her music. "Once I got into high school I became really obsessed with it," she says. "When I graduated, I went full fledged." She also became obsessed with her image, even dying her hair blonde on a dare while she was in high school. "Me, I'm very comfortable being blonde. My hair was blonde for seven years before my first album came out. I love being blonde." She also got her well-known paw-print tattoos on a dare.

———— " ————

*"I got punished a lot,"
Eve admits. "I got in trouble
for cutting school, staying
out late, lying about
detention, and lying about
homework. I hated high
school. I always knew there
was something else."*

———— " ————

After high school, Eve thought about going to college like some of her friends, but she had always dreamed of a career in music. Her mother told her to go for it while she could. She had a period of confusion, where she worked as a stripper in the Bronx for a few weeks. "I did it because it was rebellious for me to do it. . . . I realized, 'You know what? This is not what I need to be doing with my life.'" After that, she decided to get serious about her music. She had started to go out on auditions, but she would have to keep working at it to get her big break.

CAREER HIGHLIGHTS

From Dr. Dre to Ruff Ryders

With the help of some friends, Eve had the good fortune to land an audition with Dr. Dre's label, Aftermath. The audition went well, and she was flown to Los Angeles to do a demo. She signed with the label and spent eight months in L.A. working on an album, but nothing ever came of it. Eve was sent back to Philadelphia with nothing to show for it. Devastated, she "walked around my mom's house in pajamas for a whole month," she now admits. Her mother told her it would all work out for the best, and she was right. Through friendships Eve had made while she was in L.A., she got an audition with the music label Ruff Ryders, located in New York. They put her in a studio with some other rappers and told her to show them what she had. It resulted in Eve being signed as their first female rapper.

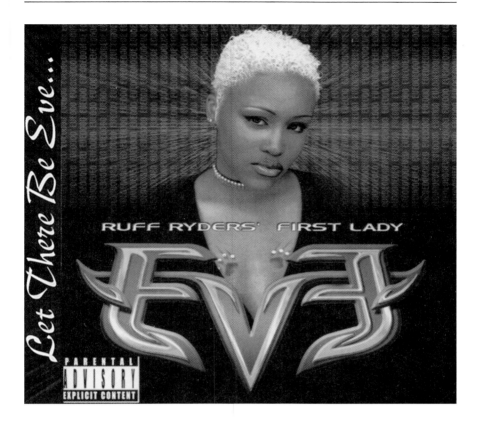

Let There Be Eve: Ruff Ryders' First Lady

Let There Be Eve: Ruff Ryders' First Lady, Eve's first album, was released in 1999. It debuted at No. 1 and eventually sold over two million copies, going multi-platinum. As a female rapper in a male-dominated field, Eve was getting a lot of attention. On one of the tracks, she described herself as a "pit bull in a skirt," and the name stuck. Fans seemed to love her defiant, in-your-face style. One reviewer said that unlike other female rappers, Eve "radiated power." Her good looks, signature blonde hair, paw-print tattoos, and fashion sense made her an instant star.

Eve's first tour was a difficult experience. When *Let There Be Eve* debuted at No. 1, the stress of almost instant fame was enormous. She fought with the friends who accompanied her on tour — they just didn't understand the pressure she was under. They wanted to party all the time, even when Eve had just finished a big performance late at night. Eve left the tour early and spent of couple of months seriously depressed. "I think everything was just so overwhelming for me. Everything happened so fast — friends, family, business associates, people, lawyers, contracts, budgets, everything. Just so much. I was 21. And there was nobody who I felt like I could really talk to, who really understood what I was going through. . . . I just crashed. I got out of it by talking to myself. I cried a lot. I prayed a lot. It was crazy. I don't ever want to go through that again, but I'm glad it happened. I learned from it."

———— " ————

"I think everything was just so overwhelming for me," Eve says about her first tour. "Everything happened so fast. . . . And there was nobody who I felt like I could really talk to, who really understood what I was going through. . . . I just crashed. I got out of it by talking to myself. I cried a lot. I prayed a lot. It was crazy. I don't ever want to go through that again, but I'm glad it happened. I learned from it."

———— " ————

Eve and her friends had always dreamed that rapping would make them rich. That dream was now a reality for her. When the first big checks arrived, she bought a mink and took some friends shopping, but she didn't do anything really crazy. Then she did some "responsible things" with her money — gave gifts to her family and bought a house and a car. She was the first woman in her family to own a house, which made her very proud. To this day, Eve continues to watch her spending. She has an accountant who manages her finances, monitors her expenses, and makes investments for the future. Eve is careful with her money, except for an occasional jewelry shopping spree, to ensure that she will be comfortable for life. She does admit, though, that she has a problem with shoes. "I am ridiculously into shoes. My accountant called me once and was like, 'What are you doing?' She put me on shoe punishment for a month."

Scorpion

Scorpion, Eve's second album, was released in 2001. The second album can be very important for a performer who has had a popular debut — it can show whether the artist has staying power. *Scorpion* had fairly good reviews and established Eve as a serious artist. "*Scorpion* is rooted in hardcore stomp, rhymes, boasts, and slams," David Browne wrote in *Entertainment Weekly*. "So much contemporary hip-hop feels sluggish and monochro-

matic, . . . [but] *Scorpion* pumps up the volume, the rhythms, everything."
As Lorraine Ali wrote in *Newsweek,* "This record is more diverse than her
debut—the formerly hard-nosed rapper now sings (and actually harmo-
nizes) atop far-flung sounds: Latin horns here, reggae melodies there. The
. . . swagger and party numbers that drove her debut still dominate, but a
more complex musical backdrop and plausible, honest lyrics about everything from the hurtful deception felt at the hands of former friends to her
disgust toward a weak boyfriend add needed substance."

In fact, *Scorpion* showed her taking some risks by moving away from the
typical Ruff Ryders' hardcore lyrics. "I think it's a good balance of the hardcore from the first album and the artist I wanna become as I get older," Eve
says. "Before, the lyrics were mine, but the vision was pretty much theirs
[from Ruff Ryder]. Like there was a song about a heist that was totally the

guys' idea. After that, I promised myself I would never make a song about shooting, robbing, anything like that, 'cause it's not me."

The album featured the hit song "Let Me Blow Ya Mind," which Eve performed with Gwen Stefani of No Doubt. (For more information on Stefani, see *Biography Today*, Sep. 2003.) The song was produced by Dr. Dre, who had dropped Eve from his Aftermath label a couple of years earlier. "I never had no animosity toward him. After a couple of months." She now thinks he is great, especially after the hit they made together, but she admits that things got a little ugly while they were working in the studio. "He's got his formula and I got mine. And we was clashin'."

Attending the Grammy Awards that year was exciting. Eve had received two Grammy nominations for *Scorpion*: she was nominated for Best Rap Album and for Best Rap/Sung Collaboration for "Let Me Blow Ya Mind." Eve attended the awards with her mother and was elated when she and Stefani won for "Let Me Blow Ya Mind." When asked about winning a Grammy, she said, "My mother was there, so she was able to share that with me. I cried, I screamed. I felt really blessed," she explains. "I never got awards in high school. So when they called my name, it was like, 'Mommy!' It was an incredible moment."

Eve-Olution

Eve's third album, called *Eve-Olution*, was released in 2002. It included several collaborations, with Snoop Dogg and Nate Dogg, Jadakiss and Styles, and Alicia Keys on the hit "Gangsta Lovin'." Eve said that the album title fit. "[I've] evolved as a person, mentally and spiritually. I think I've gotten closer to God. It's like a whole package. I've definitely grown. My ear for music has grown — you can hear it on the new album, both lyrically and musically. It's a little different from the first and second albums. I think it's more melodic."

By this point in her career, Eve was able to exert a lot more control over the album's artistic development. *Eve-Olution* was praised for its diversity of styles and influences, including reggae, rock, and gospel. Her songs on the album also reveal her interests, like relationships, men, love, or even the environment. She has been praised for speaking out against abuse toward women. "I don't listen to a lot of hip-hop anymore because I can't respect it," she admits. "Some people are gonna hate me for this, but it's like you're not busting guns anymore. We got in the business to get away from all of that. If you're gonna talk about it, at least have a moral to the story. You're not sellin' drugs anymore. It's like, 'C'mon! Talk about something else.'"

Eve-Olution gathered respect from many sources. Critic Marc Weingarten said that this album had "a fluid flow that glides effortlessly into double-time imprecations and snarling put-downs. Eve wields her new vocal weapon fearlessly, venturing into the stark noir-hop of 'What,' with its ominous staccato string section . . . before emerging into the bright daylight of 'Gangsta Lovin','" with its funky harpsichord fantasia." With three solid hit albums under her belt, Eve was ready to explore new challenges outside the music arena.

Barbershop and UPN's "Eve"

At the same time that Eve was working on *Eve-Olution*, she was already branching out into new areas. She started modeling and doing a few commercials and then made her break into film with a small part in *XXX* with Vin Diesel. It wasn't much, but it was enough to get noticed. She followed that with a role in the surprise 2002 hit *Barbershop*. This ensemble comedy is about a local barbershop that is more than a small business. Instead, it serves as the neighborhood social center—a center for gossip, for debate, for laughter, for community news, and for friendship. The shop is owned

Eve and the gang in a scene from Barbershop.

by Calvin (Ice Cube), who inherited it from his father. There are seven barbers — six males, one female, six blacks, one white — each with their own story. Eve plays Terri, a hard-edged woman who is trying but failing to leave her cheating boyfriend. When the story opens, Calvin is worried about the business and is on the verge of selling it, and the group rallies to save it.

"
"The character is very similar to me in real life," Eve said about the character Terri in **Barbershop**. *"I'm the only female involved with Ruff Ryders, so I'm used to being surrounded by testosterone all the time. I have to be tough with them the same way Terri is in the shop. She has a little bit of an attitude because she needs them to respect her."*
"

Eve's role in *Barbershop* delighted her fans and made her visible to people who hadn't noticed her before. She took her new acting career seriously, employing an acting coach and working very hard to improve her comedic skills. Eve has said that she loved playing Terri in *Barbershop*: "The character is very similar to me in real life," she says. "I'm the only female involved with Ruff Ryders, so I'm used to being surrounded by testosterone all the time. I have to be tough with them the same way Terri is in the shop. She has a little bit of an attitude because she needs them to respect her." Her performance was exactly what the director, Tim Story, had in mind for the character. "I was very adamant about getting the right person for Terri," he explains, "and when Eve came to read for us, I was interested as soon as she opened her mouth. I'd seen a lot of actresses, some of whom were phenomenal, but I was looking for somebody who was Terri, not somebody trying to be Terri. And although it's Eve's first movie role, she held her own. Her character is the only female in an all-male barbershop, so she has to show that character will stand up for herself, and she's been doing it. She gave me more than I expected every time."

The film was very successful with audiences, who enjoyed the fast-paced topical humor and the warm storyline. But *Barbershop* ultimately became controversial because some of its humor was considered offensive. The character Eddie, an elderly and outspoken barber played by Cedric the Entertainer, voices a lot of opinions that some viewers found objectionable. In particular, he disparages the civil rights icons Rosa Parks and Martin

Shelly and friends from the TV show "Eve."

Luther King, Jr., as well as other famous African Americans. That caused many civil rights leaders and others to criticize the film for its disrespectful comments — but it also led to widespread publicity and even more viewers.

In 2003, Eve made her move into the world of television with the premier of the UPN series "Eve," for which she serves as both star and co-executive producer. The show was originally titled "The Opposite Sex," but producers wanted fans to be able to identify Eve's show instantly among the dozens of other new shows that were also debuting at that time. She plays Shelly, a fashion designer living in Miami, having a good time but struggling with her relationships with men. Her two best friends — one of whom is single and gorgeous, while the other is married and out of the dating scene — try to help her navigate her way through the difficulties of balancing romance and career. While her girlfriends speak up for the female point of view, her guy friends speak up for the men. "Eve" presents a fresh and funny look at male and female relationships.

The show has been complimented for good chemistry between its characters, but it has also been called average and predictable. After a rough start that almost got it canceled, "Eve" quickly gained popularity. The show's connection with fashion was a bonus for Eve, who was already a fashion trendsetter preparing to debut her own clothing line that year. It gave her a chance to wear some of her new line in the show.

Fashion Line Fetish

It took work for Eve to expand beyond her fierce rap persona. The first images of her showed a scowling face and defiant pose. When she wanted to break into film and fashion, people were wary of her hard image. So Eve hired stylists to help her soften her look. They changed her hair and dressed her in more alluring styles, including the flowing peasant blouses that were popular at the time. The move worked; she began appearing in magazines, modeled for Tommy Hilfiger, and earned a reputation as a style trendsetter. She hoped that she could follow in the footsteps of Sean "P. Diddy" Combs, who had successfully moved from music into a number of other fields, including fashion design and restaurant ownership.

> *In 2003 Eve premiered her new clothing line, Fetish. "I am completely involved in this. Nothing gets done without my approval. I am so psychotic about it. Even down to the zipper pull. . . . This is my line. It carries my name. I have to be involved and I have to want to wear it."*

In 2003 Eve premiered her new clothing line, Fetish. Fashion had interested her since she was a child, so her entry into that world was natural. The clothing line has had excellent initial sales; they hope to move into a full line that includes everything from fragrances to eyewear at some point in the future. Eve participates in all aspects of the project. "I am completely involved in this. Nothing gets done without my approval. I am so psychotic about it. Even down to the zipper pull. . . . This is my line. It carries my name. I have to be involved and I have to want to wear it."

Recent Films

The year 2004 proved to be a busy time for Eve, with three different movies scheduled for release. First up was *Barbershop 2: Back in Business*, a sequel to the hit 2002 film. The barbershop once again is threatened, and Calvin struggles to save it. Many of the actors reprised their original roles, and they

Eve and Storm P in The Cookout.

were joined by Queen Latifah, who plays a hair stylist in a nearby shop. Eve was excited to return to the role of Terri. "I just had to come back," she says. "I had such a great time doing the first *Barbershop*, and I just fell in love with Terri. Plus, it was fun because Terri has a love interest in *Barbershop 2*, and it's someone you'd never guess." While the sequel didn't achieve quite the same level of success as the original, fans of *Barbershop* enjoyed spending more time with the crew.

Eve followed that up with *The Cookout*, another feel-good ensemble comedy. It co-starred Queen Latifah, Danny Glover, Tim Meadows, Ja Rule, Farrah Fawcett, and Storm P, who plays a young basketball player who gets a $30 million deal to play for the New Jersey Nets. Pressured by his greedy girlfriend, he buys a house in an exclusive gated community, much to the chagrin of his conservative neighbors. When he gives a cookout for his friends, family, and new neighbors, everything seems to go awry. Eve plays his childhood friend and former girlfriend, one of many people who show up to enjoy the party. Audience response was strong, although the movie was largely overlooked by critics.

Perhaps Eve's most surprising project to date is her role in *The Woodsman*, which is scheduled for release in late 2004. The movie focuses on a convicted child molester named Walter, played by Kevin Bacon. Just released after 12 years in prison and trying to make a new life for himself, he gets a job at a lumberyard. That's where he meets a co-worker, played by Kyra Sedgwick, who gives him hope for the future, but that's also where he meets Mary Kay, played by Eve, a vindictive secretary.

This was Eve's first role in a serious drama, and she made the most of it. *The Woodsman* won widespread acclaim at film festivals throughout 2004, and critics singled out Eve for praise, as in these comments from Karen Durbin in the *New York Times*. "In an important secondary role, Eve . . . gives her character such complicated powers of attraction that you find yourself checking to see what she's up to even when she's just doing her job. Her Mary Kay is smart, a bit spicy, and frankly pleased with herself—the sort of person who makes a dull workplace feel special because she has to so she can feel special herself," Durbin wrote. "One of the best things about Eve's performance is the way she shows us indignation quietly simmering into malice, all the more toxic for being sincerely self-righteous. When she starts nosing around in Walter's background, the prospect of what she'll do with all that power gives you a little thrill of dread."

Future Plans

For the future, Eve has said that she wants to continue working in music, movies, and fashion. "I see myself definitely successful in whatever it is I'm doing," she remarks. "There are so many ideas in my head. But I definitely see myself being successful and well-off, and married with children." Recently, her spiritual life has become more important to her. "Prayer is very important. Keep God first. Believe in yourself at all times, stay positive, and stay original."

HOME AND FAMILY

Eve owns a home in New Jersey. She is single. She says that she hopes to get married one day and have several children.

HOBBIES AND OTHER INTERESTS

When she isn't acting, recording, or on tour, Eve likes to shop, sleep, and watch TV and movies in her pajamas. She says she is such a lazy person that she has to force herself to keep busy. Her "babies" are her two Yorkshire terriers: Spunky is a three pound teacup, and Bear is a seven pounder who loves to get in the trash, just like a real bear. They stay with her mom when Eve is on tour.

CREDITS

CDs

Let There Be Eve: Ruff Ryders' First Lady, 1999
Scorpion, 2001
Eve-Olution, 2002

Television

"Eve," 2003- (ongoing)

Films

XXX, 2002
Barbershop, 2002
Barbershop 2: Back in Business, 2004
The Cookout, 2004
The Woodsman, 2004

HONORS AND AWARDS

Grammy Awards: 2001, for Best Rap/Sung Collaboration, for "Let Me
   Blow Ya Mind" (with Gwen Stefani)

FURTHER READING

Books

Contemporary Black Biography, Vol. 29, 2001
Contemporary Musicians, Vol. 34, 2002
Who's Who among African Americans, 2004

Periodicals

Current Biography Yearbook, 2003
Detroit Free Press, Sep. 14, 2003, p.J1
Entertainment Weekly, Mar. 9, 2001, p.78; Sep. 20, 2002, Listen2This section,
   p.16
Essence, Mar. 2004, p.142
Interview, Nov. 2000, p.155; Sep. 2002, p.192
Jet, Apr. 9, 2001, p.58; Nov. 10, 2003, p.60; Feb. 9, 2004, p.58
Los Angeles Times, Aug. 29, 1999, p.3
Newsweek, Mar. 12, 2001, p.70; Sep. 2, 2002, p.60
Philadelphia Inquirer, Sep. 14, 1999, p.E1; Nov. 9, 2003, p.M1

Rolling Stone, Oct. 28, 1999, p.44; July 5, 2001, p.58; Oct. 31, 2002, p.42; Oct. 30, 2003, p.62
Teen People, Dec. 1, 2002, p.88
Time, Mar. 19, 2001, p.74
Variety, Sep. 1, 2003, p.S18

Online Databases

Biography Resource Center Online, 2004, articles from *Contemporary Black Biography,* 2001, and *Contemporary Musicians,* 2002

ADDRESS

Eve
Universal Music Group
2200 Colorado Avenue
Santa Monica, CA 90404

WORLD WIDE WEB SITES

http://www.upn.com/shows/eve
http://www.evefans.com
http://www.fetishbyeve.com/home.php

Jennie Finch 1980-

American Softball Player
Gold Medal-Winning Pitcher for Team USA at the
2004 Summer Olympics

BIRTH

Jennie Finch was born in the Los Angeles area on September
3, 1980. Her parents are Doug Finch, a cement-truck driver
who later became a softball pitching and hitting instructor,
and Beverly Finch, a secretary at an outpatient surgery clinic.
She has two older brothers, Shane and Landon.

YOUTH

Finch grew up in a household that loved baseball. Her older brothers both played the game growing up, and Beverly Finch was a passionate fan of the Los Angeles Dodgers. In fact, she held season tickets to Dodgers games throughout Jennie's childhood. "She wasn't just like the normal person who would go to a Dodgers game," Jennie recalled. "It was like she had to be there with the radio [to listen to the broadcast of the game she was watching]."

Jennie's rise to softball stardom began when she started playing T-ball as a five-year-old. She quickly displayed an unusual talent for the game, and over the next couple of years she became one of the best players — boy or girl — in the area. By the time she was eight years old, she had switched to competitive junior softball. The following year, she began playing in distant softball tournaments as a member of various local all-star teams. "My family vacations were softball tournaments," she recalled. "Seeing the sacrifices [my parents] made growing up, understanding what they did for me and how hard it was and seeing the benefits I have from it, it's amazing."

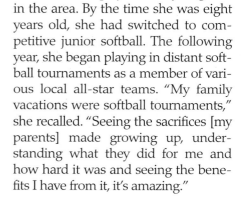

> "My family vacations were softball tournaments," Finch recalled. "Seeing the sacrifices [my parents] made growing up, understanding what they did for me and how hard it was and seeing the benefits I have from it, it's amazing."

Around this same time, Doug Finch hurt his back. Ordered by his doctor to find a less physically demanding line of work, he combined his interest in softball and his talent for working with kids to launch a business as a softball instructor. He converted the Finch backyard into a virtual instructional facility and even patented a training machine for softball pitchers that remains popular with programs around the country. Before long he had dozens of young students clamoring for instruction. But his prized pupil was his own daughter. In one interview with "NBC Nightly News," for example, he recalled an amusing incident from one of Jennie's earliest tournaments. "She was 10 years old, and she started crying out on the mound and I said, 'Jennie, what's wrong?' And she goes, 'Did you hear what that coach called me?' And I said, 'No.' And she said, 'A pitching machine!' And I said, 'Jennie, that's a compliment.'"

As the years passed, Jennie continued to develop her talents as a pitcher, fielder, and hitter. She led her local 12-and-under softball team to a national title, and by the time she reached high school she was firing fastballs that were virtually unhittable. Jennie's love for softball deepened in 1996, when she watched Team USA claim the first Olympic gold medal ever awarded in women's softball at the Summer Games in Atlanta, Georgia. "When I watched that team with [pitcher] Lisa Fernandez and [shortstop] Dot Richardson, that's where I wanted to be," she said.

Despite spending much of her youth in dusty dugouts and seemingly endless car rides, Jennie's tomboy tendencies were balanced by a taste for more traditionally feminine pastimes. "Growing up, I loved to go to the dances, I loved getting dressed up, I loved getting my makeup done and my hair done," she remembered.

EDUCATION

Finch attended La Mirada High School in La Mirada, California. One of the finest athletes in the school's history, she left her mark not only in softball, but also in volleyball and basketball. She earned varsity letters as both a junior and senior (when she was team captain) in volleyball, and she made an even bigger impact on the basketball floor. Finch served as captain of the basketball team as a senior as well, and she earned team Most Valuable Player honors her last two years of school.

——— *"* ———

Jennie's tomboy tendencies were balanced by a taste for more traditionally feminine pastimes. "Growing up, I loved to go to the dances, I loved getting dressed up, I loved getting my makeup done and my hair done," she remembered.

——— *"* ———

Still, softball remained Finch's best sport throughout high school. Named to the varsity team as a freshman, she rewrote the school's record books in the sport. By the time she had completed her high school career, she had compiled a 50-12 record as a pitcher, including 13 no-hitters, a 0.15 earned run average (ERA), and 784 strikeouts in 445 innings pitched. Displaying a rare combination of pitching talent and hitting power, she earned league Most Valuable Player honors in both her junior and senior years. Most impressively, she led La Mirada to four consecutive league championships—the last as captain of the team—while splitting time between the pitcher, shortstop, and first base positions.

By the time Finch graduated in 1998, she was acknowledged as one of the top softball prospects in the entire country. *Jump Magazine,* in fact, ranked her as the top softball recruit in the nation. Scholarship offers poured in

Finch's 2001 season was perhaps the greatest ever for a pitcher in NCAA softball history.

from a wide assortment of college programs, but in the end Finch decided to join the powerhouse softball program at the University of Arizona in Tucson. Four years later, in 2002, she graduated with a communications degree — and a fistful of NCAA records and honors.

CAREER HIGHLIGHTS

College — University of Arizona Wildcats

Finch made an immediate splash as a freshman at Arizona. "Jennie is just an awesome player," said one of her older teammates. "She can pitch, she can play infield, and she can hit for power." Most importantly, Finch showed resilience and determination when things didn't go her way. At the outset of the season, she was hit hard by a few opposing teams, but by season's end she was one of the team's top pitchers. "The biggest adjustment [from high school to college] has been not dealing with just batters one through four [in the nine-person batting line-up] being good, but the whole line-up being strong," she said. Finch's pitching and hitting helped lift the Wildcats all the way to the NCAA Softball World Series before they were defeated.

In the summer of 1999 Finch earned a silver medal with USA Softball at the Junior Women's World Championships. She then returned to Arizona for her sophomore campaign. As the season unfolded, it became clear to teammates and opponents alike that Finch had pushed her game to a new and more dominant level. By season's end she had posted a remarkable 29-2 pitching record, while also batting .327 and whacking 16 home runs, tied for best on the team. She continued her terrific performance in the postseason, earning NCAA Regional Most Outstanding Player honors on the strength of her 3-0 record and 0.35 ERA. Once again, her clutch pitching and hitting helped the Wildcats advance to the World Series before falling.

In 2001 Finch delivered perhaps the greatest season by a pitcher in NCAA softball history. At season's end she had a 32-0 record—an NCAA record for most victories in a season without a defeat. She also finished the season with a .309 batting average and 11 home runs, including 3 grand slams.

Then, after helping Arizona reach the World Series for a third straight year, she lifted the team to the championship by throwing a four-hitter against the UCLA Lady Bruins for a 1-0 victory. In recognition of her stellar season, Finch easily won the 2001 Honda Award, presented each year to the best college softball player in the country.

"Everyone always talks about how good-looking she is," admitted Arizona head coach Mike Candrea. "But Jennie Finch is a fierce competitor. . . . She also wants to be known for what she does on the field."

As Finch prepared for her senior season, she was surprised to find that the public spotlight was beginning to shine on her. Part of this attention was due to her amazing softball skills, but virtually everyone agreed that it also stemmed from her striking ap-

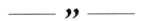

pearance. "Everyone always talks about how good-looking she is," admitted Arizona head coach Mike Candrea. "But Jennie Finch is a fierce competitor. . . . She also wants to be known for what she does on the field."

In 2002 Finch continued her dominant performance on the mound, extending her winning streak to an NCAA-record 60 games. Riding her blazing softballs to victory after victory, the Wildcats advanced once again to the season-ending College World Series, where their bid for a second consecutive championship fell short. This disappointment did not detract from Finch's incredible season, though. Once again, her exploits brought her the Honda Award.

Finch's incredible career at the Universita of Arizona will not soon be forgotten. In fact, her jersey number 27 was permanently retired by the team on May 9, 2003, in recognition of her years of excellence on the softball diamond.

Finch's pre-game jitters didn't show when she took the field at the 2004 Olympics.

After graduating from Arizona, Finch turned her attention to international competition. As a pitcher and first baseman for the U.S. national women's softball squad, she helped clinch a gold medal in the 2002 World Championships. One year later, she earned a gold medal as part of the victorious American team at the Pan American Games. It came as no surprise to anyone when she was named to the squad that would compete at the 2004 Summer Olympics in Athens, Greece.

Keeping Good Looks in Perspective

As the 2004 Olympics approached, American media outlets flocked to Finch's side like never before. Finch recognized that, as in college, the attention from television and magazine outlets was due at least as much to her appearance as her athletic skills.

Finch worked hard to keep this attention in perspective. She never sought to hide her looks or pretend that it was not a factor in her growing popularity. On the contrary, she recognized that the attention gave her an opportunity to improve her financial future through endorsements and personal appearances. For that reason, she willingly appeared on such shows as "Best Damn Sports Show, Period," and "The Late Show with David Letterman." She also agreed to appear in a regular segment on "This Week in

Baseball," in which she pitched against major league stars. Finally, she cooperated with various magazines that wanted to feature her in stories about the upcoming Olympic Games.

At the same time, however, Finch never embarrassed herself or her teammates in the gathering pre-Olympic excitement. For example, she repeatedly turned down lucrative magazine offers to pose for photographs that were blatantly sexual in tone. She said that these offers never tempted her, partly because of her strong religious beliefs and partly because she felt that she would be letting teammates and fans down. "I had a lot more to lose than to gain," she stated. "I'm a role model for lots of young girls."

Finch also tried to make sure that the attention surrounding her advanced the sport of softball and helped her teammates gain greater recognition. "Whatever magazine I'm in, or we're in, we're excited because it does help softball," she stated. "I don't know how comfortable I am with the whole sex-symbol thing. I don't see myself that way. But it has helped the sport grow. I think it changes how people see women's athletics. For a long time, it wasn't cool or hip to be a woman and be a female athlete. Now, being athletic is the in thing to do. Athletic women are sexy now, whereas in the past they weren't."

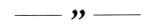

"I don't know how comfortable I am with the whole sex-symbol thing. I don't see myself that way. But it has helped the sport grow. I think it changes how people see women's athletics. For a long time, it wasn't cool or hip to be a woman and be a female athlete. Now, being athletic is the in thing to do. Athletic women are sexy now, whereas in the past they weren't."

Finch's teammates seemed to appreciate the efforts she took to handle the attention with grace. "It's amazing how she takes all the attention in stride," said teammate Stacey Nuveman. "It's not something she thinks about or worries about. It doesn't affect her at all, and that's a special thing." "If she was bad, it would be completely different," added teammate Lori Harrigan. "You do have to take the publicity when you can get it, but at the same time it's too bad our society looks at Jennie as beautiful first, and a great pitcher second. . . . We have so many great players who don't get the recognition and if it's because of what they look like then that is too bad. But at the same time, if you have somebody who is good at what they do and is beautiful and people want to publicize it, then so be it."

Preparing for Athens

In the spring of 2004 the USA women's softball team went on a long pre-Olympics tour of the country, taking on a variety of top college teams and various all-star squads. The team went undefeated, usually romping by lop-sided scores. Finch herself posted a 15-0 mark with a 0.27 ERA during the tour. The squad thus went to Athens brimming with confidence. "We want to experience that gold-medal experience," Finch said. "Anything less is unacceptable."

> "*Walking out onto the field [at the Olympics], seeing thousands of young girls waving American flags" made her feel invincible, Finch later said. "I've dreamed of being an Olympian since I was little. And suddenly it was a reality.*"

Team USA was the heavy favorite in the softball competition. Experts agreed that the team's strong batting line-up — combined with an overpowering pitching staff led by Finch and Olympic veteran Lisa Fernandez — made them the team to beat. Still, Finch admitted that she was very nervous in the hours before the opening game. "This is a game I've been playing since I was five years old," she said. "I was telling myself you can't get too high or too low, but you can only do so much of that talking. It's the Olympics."

When Finch took the field to pitch, though, she felt a sudden surge of confidence. "Walking out onto the field, seeing thousands of young girls waving American flags" made her feel invincible, she later said. "I've dreamed of being an Olympian since I was little. And suddenly it was a reality."

Rolling to Gold

Team USA cruised through the opening rounds in Athens, with Finch and other pitchers posting four consecutive one-hit shutouts. In the meantime, the Americans' bats exploded for 31 runs during that span. Finch and her teammates continued to roll in the medal round, shutting out every opponent to reach the gold medal game against Australia. "This is absolutely the best Olympic team the U.S. has fielded and if you make one mistake you're done," declared Canadian coach Mike Renney.

In the gold medal game the Australians finally ended Team USA's string of shutouts, scratching out a single run. But it was not enough, as the Ameri-

Team USA was elated to win the gold medal at the 2004 Olympics. From left: Lisa Fernandez, Leah Amico, Lori Harrigan, and Jennie Finch.

cans knocked in five runs to claim Olympic gold. From that point forward, Finch savored every moment of the Olympics, from the medal ceremony to the closing ceremonies. "It was awesome," she told "Good Morning America." "It was the most incredible feeling standing up on that podium with my teammates, celebrating in this gold medal." Finch hopes to experience it all again in 2008, when she hopes to compete in the Olympics with the U.S. team.

HOME AND FAMILY

Finch is engaged to Casey Daigle, a pitcher with the Arizona Diamondbacks organization. She has said that she'd eventually like to have four or five children.

HOBBIES AND OTHER INTERESTS

Finch loves to relax by going shopping. In addition to her continued involvement with the Team USA softball program, she has signed promotional deals with a number of companies.

HONORS AND AWARDS

NCAA Regional Most Outstanding Player: 1999, 2000
First-Team All-American (NCCA): 2000, 2001, 2002
First-Team All Pacific-10 (PAC-10): 2000, 2001, 2002

Most Outstanding Player, NCAA Women's College World Series: 2001
Honda Award (as best collegiate softball player): 2001, 2002
PAC-10 Pitcher of the Year: 2001, 2002
International Softball Federation World Championships: gold medal, 2002
Pan American Games: gold medal, 2004
Olympic Women's Softball: gold medal, 2004

FURTHER READING

Periodicals

Arizona Daily Star, May 24, 2001, p.C1
Business Week, Aug. 2, 2004, p.61
Cincinnati Post, July 5, 2004, p.C1
Current Biography Yearbook, 2004
Glamour, July 2004, p.215
Grand Rapids (Mich.) Press, Aug. 17, 2004, p.F12
New York Post, May 14, 2004, p.88
New York Times, Aug. 8, 2004, p.L3; Aug. 15, 2004, p.SP4
Philadelphia Inquirer, June 29, 2004, p.F1
Rocky Mountain News, July 17, 2004, p.B1
Sports Illustrated, Aug. 23, 2004, p.32
Sports Illustrated Women, Mar./Apr. 2002, p.32
USA Today, Feb. 13, 2004, p.C15; Aug. 10, 2004, p.A1; Aug. 19, 2004, p.D4
Washington Post, June 22, 2003, p.E1

Online Articles

Additional information for this profile was obtained from the transcripts of "Good Morning America" (Aug. 24, 2004), "NBC Nightly News" (Aug. 23, 2004), and "Today" (May 24, 2004).

ADDRESS

Jennie Finch
USA Softball
2801 NE 50th Street
Oklahoma City, OK 73111-7203

WORLD WIDE WEB SITES

http://www.jenniefinch.net
http://www.usasoftball.com

Wally Funk 1939-

American Aviation Pioneer
Member of the Historic "Mercury 13" Group of
Female Astronaut Candidates

BIRTH

Mary Wallace Funk—who insists on being called "Wally"—
was born on January 31, 1939, in Taos, New Mexico. Her parents, Lozier and Virginia Funk, owned a five-and-dime store
in Taos. She had one older brother, Clark, who was born in
1936.

―――― **"** ――――

"I grew up in an area where you had free spirit,"
Funk said. "[Indian friends] taught me how to fish and hunt and camp at a very early age, and survive the wilderness. So I had all that going for myself. . . . That's why I thank the good Lord for putting me where he put me."

―――― **"** ――――

YOUTH

Funk first explored the wonders of flight as a five-year-old. It was then that she took to jumping from the roof of the family barn into waiting haystacks, a Superman cape clasped around her neck. These jumping stunts reflected the fun and carefree nature of Funk's childhood. When she wasn't selling rabbits, squash, strawberries, corn, and arrowheads to tourists outside her father's store, she could usually be found exploring the wild country outside Taos with friends from a local Tiwa Indian tribe. "I grew up in an area where you had free spirit," she said. "[Indian friends] taught me how to fish and hunt and camp at a very early age, and survive the wilderness. So I had all that going for myself, where a youngster today is in a city, in an apartment, and that's all they know. They don't know ocean and skiing and snow and air as I was able to know it, and that's why I thank the good Lord for putting me where he put me."

As Wally grew older, she developed a strong fascination with machines — and especially airplanes. "Mother wanted a froufrou girl with frills, and all I wanted was an Erector set," she recalled. When it became clear that Wally's interest in planes was not a passing fancy, though, both of her parents were very supportive. Her father brought home model airplanes for her to build, and her mother drove her out to the tiny local airport to watch the planes come and go. By the time she was a teenager, Wally's hero was Amelia Earhart, a famous American aviator who disappeared over the Pacific Ocean during a 1937 flight.

Wally later learned that her mother's encouragement stemmed from her own experiences as a young woman. After taking a ride with a "barnstormer" — a stunt flyer who performs at county fairs and carnivals — Virginia Funk burst into her home talking excitedly about learning to fly. But her hopes were immediately shot down by her father. "He told her that she would become a fine young woman, a good wife, and an excellent mother," reported Wally. "And she was all of those things. But she also passed along those flying genes to me, and she supported me all the way."

Wally's love for adventure and the outdoors took other forms, too. She became an expert rifle marksman, receiving the Distinguished Rifleman's Award at age 14. She also competed in various slalom and downhill skiing competitions throughout the West until a serious back injury forced her to hang up her skis.

EDUCATION

Funk attended schools in the Taos area until age 16, when she enrolled at Stephens College in Columbia, Missouri. This two-year college, one of the oldest women's colleges in the country, offered several aviation courses. Not surprisingly, Funk wasted little time in signing up.

Funk made her first flight in a single-engine, four-seat airplane with her teacher and one other student. "What impressed me the most was that the airplane just kind of took itself off, and the ground was so beautifully packaged as north, south, east, west—it was all field we flew over, near the Missouri River," she remembered. "The earth was so pristine, and I was up there looking down at the perfect pattern on the ground, at the cows and the cars and the houses and the river and the town. The bug bit and that was it."

Afterward, Funk's parents agreed to pay for flight lessons for their excited daughter. Years later, she discovered that paying for her lessons constituted a major financial burden for her parents. But despite the expense, they remained steadfast in encouraging her to pursue her flying dreams.

Funk made her first solo flight at age 16 and earned her pilot's license at age 17. She then joined the Flying Susies, the intercollegiate flying squad at Stephens College. She loved the hours she spent in training flights and flying competitions, but sometimes even all this flying action was not enough to satisfy her. On one occasion, she remembered, "I snuck out the window

"What impressed me the most was that the airplane just kind of took itself off, and the ground was so beautifully packaged as north, south, east, west—it was all field we flew over, near the Missouri River," Funk remembered. "The earth was so pristine, and I was up there looking down at the perfect pattern on the ground, at the cows and the cars and the houses and the river and the town. The bug bit and that was it."

Funk was the top female pilot with the Flying Aggies for two years.

from a formal [dance] one time to go night flying and snuck back in by midnight so I wasn't caught."

In 1958 Funk graduated from Stephens College with an associate of arts degree. That same year, she received the Outstanding Female Pilot Trophy at the National Intercollegiate Flying Meet in Minneapolis, Minnesota. Most of the other awards handed out at the meet, however, went to members of the Oklahoma State University Flying Aggies.

Funk was so impressed by the Flying Aggies that she decided she had to fly with them. She subsequently enrolled at Oklahoma State, and by the close of 1959 she was one of the school's top female flyers. Meanwhile, she continued her studies in both aviation and education. By the time she graduated with a bachelor of science degree in secondary education in 1960, she had also qualified to pilot a wide variety of aircraft, from single-engine seaplanes to commercial planes.

FIRST JOBS

After graduation, Funk worked to get a job as a commercial pilot. But she was turned down flat by all the airlines, none of which had ever had a female pilot on their payroll (the first female commercial pilot in the United States was not hired until 1973). "I was told by United and Continental Airlines I couldn't be hired as a commercial pilot because there were no ladies' bathrooms in the training facilities," she recalled with a mixture of amusement and sadness.

With that avenue blocked, Funk went to Fort Sill, Oklahoma, where at age 20 she became the first civilian flight instructor of noncommissioned and commissioned officers in the history of the U.S. military. She was limited to teaching flying on propeller-driven aircraft, though, since the U.S. military did not allow women to operate jets in that era.

CAREER HIGHLIGHTS

As Funk carried out her work at Fort Sill, she—like millions of other Americans—followed with great interest the accelerating "space race" between the United States and the Communist-led Union of Soviet Socialist Republics (USSR), also known as the Soviet Union. Both nations desperately wanted to be the first to achieve certain landmarks, like putting a man on the moon. This race for supremacy was also waged in the development of nuclear weapons and economic and political power, and it dominated news coverage of the era.

"I was told by United and Continental Airlines I couldn't be hired as a commercial pilot because there were no ladies' bathrooms in the training facilities,"Funk recalled with a mixture of amusement and sadness.

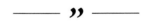

The modern age of space exploration began in 1957 when the Soviet Union launched Sputnik I, the first satellite sent into space. The United States became determined to beat the Russians in developing its space program. In 1958, the United States founded the National Aeronautics and Space Administration (NASA), which screened over 580 military pilots who had expressed interest in becoming astronauts. During the screening process, 159 pilots were selected to undergo a series of challenging physical and psychological tests. The seven men with the highest scores became the "Mercury 7" —seven astronauts who led America's first expeditions into space.

Training to Be an Astronaut

In 1960 Funk was leafing through an issue of *Life* magazine when she came across an article describing a budding NASA plan to train female astronauts. This news stunned and excited Funk, who promptly wrote a letter to the director of the fledgling program, Dr. W. Randolph Lovelace II. She boldly asked for a spot in the program, then backed up her request with a listing of her credentials, including her various collegiate flight team awards, flight instructor training, and 3,000 flying hours — over three times the number of hours Lovelace was seeking from candidates.

Impressed by Funk's ambition and aviation experience, Lovelace agreed to place her in the "Women in Space" program, which had the support — but not the official sponsorship — of NASA. Funk and 24 other women began the program in February 1961. Of all the candidates in the program, Funk was the youngest.

———— " ————

"The [sensory deprivation] tank was a piece of cake," Funk later said. *"The only thing that really hurt was when they injected freezing water into my ear [to trigger disorientation]. Now that was really painful. But I wanted to go into space so badly, I would have endured anything."*

———— " ————

The testing program, which was identical to the one used on the male astronaut candidates, was divided into three phases. Phase one consisted of 87 different tests to check physical health. Some of these tests were very unpleasant. For example, Funk and the others were forced to swallow three feet of rubber hose for a stomach test, and on another occasion 18 needles were stuck in each of their heads to record brain waves. They even were forced to consume glasses of radioactive water. "I just gulped it down," Funk recalled. "I can't say it really bothered me."

The second phase involved a combination of psychological and psychiatric testing. For many prospective astronauts — both male and female — the most disorienting and frightening of these tests was the isolation tank. In this test, candidates were placed in a pitch-black tank of warm water that was constructed to completely eliminate input for all five senses. Even the water in which the subjects floated could not be felt, since the water temperature was perfectly matched to the body temperature of each participant.

This sensory deprivation test was designed to create a feeling of weightlessness such as one might feel in space, but it also commonly caused prospective astronauts to lapse into uncontrollable hallucinations. Funk, however, never succumbed to hallucinations. Instead, she spent 10 hours and 35 minutes in the tank without hallucinating, a longer period of time than any

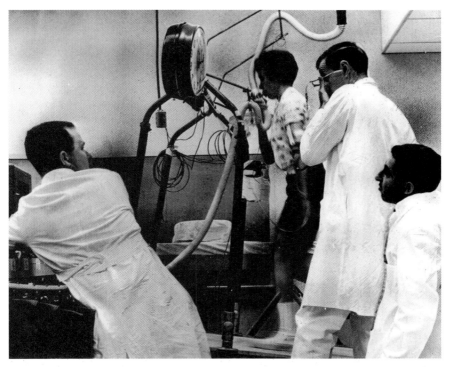

For the Mercury 13 astronaut training program, Funk underwent a series of physical, psychological, and psychiatric tests.

other man or woman who participated. "The tank was a piece of cake," she later said. "The only thing that really hurt was when they injected freezing water into my ear [to trigger disorientation]. Now that was really painful. But I wanted to go into space so badly, I would have endured anything."

Phase three of the training program was conducted at different test sites. During this process, Funk and the other astronaut candidates were tested for their reactions to high altitudes, fierce gravitational forces, and other potential elements of the space environment. "I did whatever they asked without asking questions," she said. "We hadn't been to space yet, so there was no idea what the human body would have to endure in terms of stress. That's why they tested us to the limit."

A Dream Deferred

Funk and 12 other women—dubbed the "Mercury 13"—passed the battery of tests. In fact, one doctor who helped test the women told *National*

Geographic Online that "their results were so astonishing that, at the time, I didn't see how NASA could turn them down. All of the Mercury women were extraordinary."

Nonetheless, the so-called Mercury 13 program was abruptly terminated by NASA, just when Funk and the other women had come to believe that their dream of space flight might actually come true. Director Lovelace and other Mercury 13 supporters strenuously objected to the decision, but they were told that the U.S. government had decided that America was not ready for female astronauts. "It was the era when women were in the kitchen," explained Funk. "[It was] terrible. I mean, they never gave us a chance to prove ourselves."

> ———— " ————
>
> *The so-called Mercury 13 program was abruptly terminated by NASA when the U.S. government decided that America was not ready for female astronauts. "It was the era when women were in the kitchen," explained Funk. "[It was] terrible. I mean, they never gave us a chance to prove ourselves."*
>
> ———— " ————

Funk and the other Mercury 13 members held out hope that NASA might eventually reconsider its decision. "I thought, 'Wally, you're still going into space, just not right now,'" she recalled. But in 1963, Congressional hearings conducted to study the feasibility of sending women into space determined that all astronauts should be military jet pilots. Since the U.S. military did not let women fly military jets at that time, the decision effectively killed all hopes.

Breaking New Ground in Aviation Circles

After the Mercury 13 program was suspended, Funk accepted a position in the fall of 1961 as a flight instructor and pilot with an aviation company in Hawthorne, California. She also continued her education, rising to new heights of her profession with each passing year. In 1971, for example, Funk became the first woman to successfully complete the Federal Aviation Administration's General Aviation Operations Inspector Academy course. This accomplishment qualified her to test pilots for flight certification and investigate flight violations, accidents, and other aspects of plane operation.

In 1973 Funk became the first woman in the United States to hold the position of specialist in the FAA's Systems Worthiness Analysis Program. In

In about 1961 or 1962, Funk flew this Cessna 310 as a flight instructor and pilot with an aviation company.

the ensuing months she became an inspector of both flight schools and air taxi operations. In December 1974 Funk relocated to Washington, D.C., where she became one of the first female air accident investigators in the history of the National Transportation Safety Board (NTSB). Over the next decade, she investigated more than 450 airplane accidents across the country.

The task of investigating accidents — especially fatal airplane crashes — could be a very depressing one. But it never eroded Funk's love for avia-tion. In fact, she participated in several air races across the American West in the 1970s and 1980s. Her biggest triumph in this sport came on October 4, 1975. On that day, Funk flew a red and white Citabria plane to victory over a field of 80 competitors in the Pacific Air Race, a contest that took competitors from San Diego to Santa Rosa, California.

In 1985 Funk left the NTSB. She spent the next several years working as a flight instructor and promoting flight safety at conferences and other events around the world. Funk has estimated that her work as a sort of "goodwill ambassador" for flying took her to more than 50 countries in Europe, the Middle East, and Africa. These activities put her in the public spotlight, and she has since been profiled on numerous television and radio programs and in several national publications.

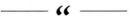

Watching Female Astronauts Make History

As Funk grew older, she continued to follow the U.S. space program with great interest. In 1983 she celebrated when Sally Ride became the first American female astronaut to go into space (the first female astronaut in the world was Valentina Tereshkova, who was part of a 1963 Soviet space flight). Twelve years later, Funk became just as excited when American Eileen Collins became the first female astronaut to serve as pilot on a space shuttle mission.

> *"Wally should have been the first woman in space, she could have been the first woman in space," said Randa Milliron, Chief Executive Officer of IOS. "Wally is the most qualified person in the world for this as well. You want somebody who can think on her feet for an activity like this. So when I fly, I want to fly with Wally."*

In a gesture of appreciation for their trailblazing efforts three decades earlier, Collins invited all surviving members of the Mercury 13 group to be her guests at the launch. It was an emotional day for Funk, who still harbored dreams of going into space. As the rocket left the launchpad, Funk felt tears streaming down her cheeks as she yelled, "Go Eileen! Go for all of us!" Collins's historic flight signaled an end to the days when women astronauts were kept to the sidelines of space flight.

Today, female astronauts are part of virtually every space shuttle crew, serving as commanders, pilots, and scientists. But Funk knew that her age made it highly unlikely that she would ever fulfill her dream of space flight on a NASA mission. In fact, NASA has rejected Funk's application to join its astronaut program four times over the years.

Certified to fly more than 30 types of airplanes, Funk continued to work as a flight instructor. She also continued to give motivational speeches to women's organizations, college groups, aviation conferences, and other

*Funk and other Mercury 13 astronaut candidates watched the
1995 launch when Eileen Collins became the first female astronaut
to pilot a space shuttle mission.*

gatherings. Her public pronouncements have drawn fire from some critics,
who accuse her of exaggerations and excessive boastfulness in her recol-
lections of her Mercury 13 days. Funk, though, says that she pays no attention to these complaints.

Moreover, Funk continued to explore alternative ways of getting into
space. In 2000, for example, she paid a hefty fee to train at the Yuri Gagarin
Cosmonaut Training Center in Russia's Space City complex. She had
hoped that these sessions might lead to an opportunity to visit the Russian
Space Station Mir orbiting above the earth. In March 2001, however, the
aging satellite—which had housed dozens of astronauts over the previous
decade—was brought back to Earth in a controlled crash.

Since that time, Funk has become involved with a privately funded aerospace corporation called Interorbital Systems (IOS), based in Mojave, California. Founded in 1996, IOS is developing commercial rocket systems for
spaceflight in hopes of launching a profitable "space tourism" business. For
the past several years, the company has been working to develop Solaris X,
a rocket capable of carrying people into orbit. In fact, the Solaris X vehicle

was entered in the Ansari X Prize, a privately financed international commercial spaceflight competition. This contest, organized by aerospace entrepreneur Peter Diamandis, offered a $10 million prize to the first team that could send a rocket carrying three people to the threshold of space — about 60 miles from Earth — and return them safely, then duplicate the feat in the same spacecraft within two weeks.

In 2002 Interorbital Systems announced that it had reached an agreement with Funk for her to pilot the Solaris X went it goes into space. "Wally should have been the first woman in space, she could have been the first woman in space," said Randa Milliron, Chief Executive Officer of IOS. "Wally is the most qualified person in the world for this as well. You want somebody who can think on her feet for an activity like this. So when I fly, I want to fly with Wally."

—————— **"** ——————

"I want to be in space in the worst way," Funk said. "I've tried in every way to kick a lot of doors in. I still have the heart of that 20-year-old. . . . What I am already dreaming about is the roar of the take-off, followed by the absolute silence as we go into orbit, and then seeing Earth outside my window."

—————— 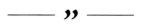 ——————

For her part, Funk expressed great excitement about the flight, which is scheduled to take place in late 2004 or 2005. "I want to be in space in the worst way," she said. "I've tried in every way to kick a lot of doors in. I still have the heart of that 20-year-old. . . . What I am already dreaming about is the roar of the take-off, followed by the absolute silence as we go into orbit, and then seeing Earth outside my window."

Unfortunately, the Interorbital Systems flight will not win the Ansari X Prize. That honor went to the American Mojave Aerospace Team, which was led by research aircraft developer Burt Rutan and financier Paul Allen. The team completed two successful suborbital space flights — on September 29 and October 4, 2004 — and was awarded the $10 million prize. But Interorbital Systems later announced that it is continuing its plans to open the space frontier to tourists. Interorbital is currently constructing two new rockets: the Nano, which will send tiny satellites into orbit, and the Neptune, a rocket capable of ferrying up to eight people into orbit. The team plans to compete for the America's Space Prize that is being offered by entrepreneur Bob Bigelow for a private vehicle that can carry passengers to orbit Earth.

HOME AND FAMILY

Funk, who has never been married, lives in Roanoke, Texas, in a home that is heavily decorated with model airplanes, flight-related ribbons and awards, and photographs documenting her decades as an aviator.

HOBBIES AND OTHER INTERESTS

Funk enjoys restoring antique automobiles and participating in firearm shooting competitions. She has also engaged in a wide variety of "extreme" sports over the years, including parachuting, bungee jumping, ballooning, and hang gliding.

HONORS AND AWARDS

Outstanding Female Pilot (National Intercollegiate Flying Meet): 1958
Pacific Air Race: 1975, First Place
International Hall of Fame for Pioneer Women in Aviation: 1995

FURTHER READING

Books

Ackmann, Martha. *The Mercury 13,* 2003
Nolen, Stephanie. *Promised the Moon: The Untold Story of the First Women in the Space Race,* 2002

Periodicals

Chicago Tribune, Feb. 1, 1995, p.C2
Dallas Morning News, Mar. 27, 1995, p.A1
Fort Worth (Tex.) Star-Telegram, Nov. 20, 1996, Metro, p.1; Sep. 25, 1999, Metro, p.1
Life, Aug. 29, 1963, p.72; June 28, 1963, p.31
Los Angeles Times Magazine, Jan. 18, 2004, p.16
People, July 7, 2003, p.114
Weekly Reader (senior edition), Apr. 2, 2004, p.2

Online Articles

http://www.houstonchron.com
(*HoustonChronicle.com,* "Wally Funk Is Still Determined to Get Her Shot at Space," Feb. 11, 2000)

http://www.guardian.co.uk
  (*Guardian Unlimited,* "Space Cowgirl," Apr. 2, 2002)
http://www.scottsdalejournal.com
  (*Scottsdale Journal Online,* "Wally Funk — From Cowgirl to Space Girl,"
  Feb. 2003)
http://www.nationalgeographic.com
  (*National Geographic.com,* "Mercury 13's Wally Funk Fights for Her Place
  in Space," July 9, 2003)

Additional information for this biographical profile was gathered from transcripts of NASA's Oral History project.

ADDRESS

Wally Funk
Interorbital Systems
P.O. Box 662
Mojave, CA 93502-0662

WORLD WIDE WEB SITES

http://www.ninety-nines.org
http://www.interorbital.com

T.D. Jakes 1957-

American Minister, Author, Broadcaster, and
Community Advocate
Pastor of The Potter's House and CEO of The Potter's
House Ministries

BIRTH

Thomas Dexter Jakes was born in South Charleston, West Virginia, on June 9, 1957. His father, Ernest Sr., was the owner of a custodial service. His mother, Odith, was a schoolteacher. He was the youngest of three children.

YOUTH

Jakes's religious faith has been an important part of his life for as long as he can remember. He loved going to the local Baptist church as a boy, and when he got home he spent hours preaching to imaginary congregations. "We were all brought up in the church," his older brother Ernest told the *Dallas Morning News*. "But it stuck with him. With me, I would go outside and play. He would want to read the Bible and go to choir practice." Jakes's enthusiasm for worship and religious study eventually became so widely known around the community that folks started calling him "Bible Boy."

> "*That's how I grew up, sleeping in waiting rooms and hospitals, suspended between life and death,*" *Jakes recalled about his father's long battle with illness.* "*And riding an emotional roller coaster at a time that I desperately needed the solidarity of my father's hand and the attention of my mother. My mother was distracted with my father, and my father was distracted with death.*"

In addition to exploring his religious faith, Jakes spent a lot of time helping out around the house. He learned to cook and sew, and he earned extra money for the family by delivering newspapers and selling Avon products. These extra dollars became vital in the late 1960s, when Ernest Jakes Sr. developed a serious kidney ailment that eventually took his life. Jakes was 10 years old when his father first became ill, and he has described the five years of suffering that his father endured before his death as a nightmare for the whole family. It also left him with an enduring respect for the pain and suffering that afflict countless people every day. "That's how I grew up, sleeping in waiting rooms and hospitals, suspended between life and death," he recalled. "And riding an emotional roller coaster at a time that I desperately needed the solidarity of my father's hand and the attention of my mother. My mother was distracted with my father, and my father was distracted with death."

EDUCATION

Jakes dropped out of high school two months before graduation to help care for his family. He eventually passed a high school equivalency exam, then enrolled as a part-time student at West Virginia State College in

Charleston. He took several psychology courses at West Virginia State. By this point he had started a part-time ministry, however, and his academic studies gradually fell by the wayside.

Jakes later resumed his education at Friends International Christian University, a correspondence school located in Merced, California. He eventually earned a bachelor's degree, a master's degree, and a doctoral degree from the school. "It's for guys like me who have already gone on [with their careers] and are halfway up the hill," he explained. "They take credits you have accrued from school and experience and round out with courses until you are eligible for a diploma."

CAREER HIGHLIGHTS

Jakes's career as a minister began in 1979, when he founded a small storefront church in Montgomery, West Virginia. This church, called the Greater Emmanuel Temple of Faith, had only ten members when it first opened its doors. But Jakes's energetic leadership seemed to bring in a trickle of new members with each passing month.

The part-time post fulfilled Jakes's need to share his faith, but it did not provide him with the money he needed to support a family. In 1981 he married Serita A. Jameson and took a factory job with Union Carbide, but the plant closed down a year later. Unable to find another stable job, Jakes dug ditches and took odd jobs for several months.

After a while, however, the Greater Emmanuel Temple of Faith expanded to the point that it was able to pay Jakes a full-time salary for his pastoral activities. This development freed him to focus all his attention on his ministry. He started a local radio program called "The Master's Plan," and in 1987 he was ordained as a bishop by Dr. Quander L. Wilson, presiding Bishop of Greater Emmanuel Apostolic Churches. Although Jakes resigned from that denomination two years later, he maintained a relationship with a small fellowship of churches collectively known as the Higher Ground Always Abounding Assemblies.

Emerging as a Gifted Counselor to Women

In 1990 Jakes moved his growing church to South Charleston, West Virginia. At the time of the move, the congregation numbered only 100 or so, but within three years the church membership tripled in size. It was during this period that Jakes developed a Sunday school lesson plan specifically tailored to address the pain and sadness he saw in many of the church's women. "I was counseling married couples and started to see that behind

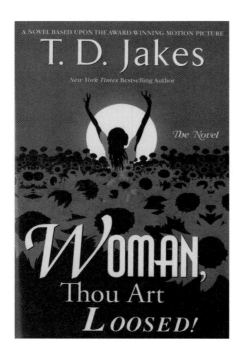

the perfect exterior were a lot of women dealing with the same problems of oppression," he recalled. "I called them all together. Part of healing is knowing that others have been through it."

Jakes was profoundly moved by the number of women in his congregation who seemed to take comfort from his program. Determined to help women deal with their emotional pain, he wrote and self-published a book called *Woman, Thou Art Loosed!* In this 1993 work, Jakes emphasized the universality of the experiences of women and urged them to take pride in their worth and responsibility for their happiness. The book proved enormously popular, and over time it became the foundation of an entire "Woman, Thou Art Loosed!" program devised by Jakes. This program—which includes audiotapes, books, and symposiums—also was instrumental in building his reputation as a skilled minister to poor, depressed, and unhappy women of all ages, races, and economic backgrounds.

Jakes's ministry continued to grow in other ways as well. In 1993 his weekly services began appearing on the Trinity Broadcasting Network. The same year, he moved his church to Cross Lanes, West Virginia. Before long, his congregation grew to about 1,100 members. About 40 percent of the congregation was white, an unusually high percentage for a church led by a black pastor.

In 1994 Jakes expanded his television ministry to Black Entertainment Television (BET). Two years later, he made the biggest move of his career, relocating his ministry to Dallas, Texas. Jakes later admitted that moving to the Dallas area was scary in some respects. "We literally felt like the Beverly Hillbillies coming out of West Virginia to a place where I couldn't get out of [Dallas/Fort Worth] Airport effectively," he said. "It was an adventure." But the move gave Jakes the resources he needed to bring his ministry to a whole new level. Accompanied by 50 staff members and their families from West Virginia, Jakes settled into a huge, modern church located on a compound of about 30 acres. This ideal property had become available after the previous occupant, a televangelist, had been imprisoned for tax evasion.

Founding the Potter's House

Jakes decided to name his nondenominational church The Potter's House — a tribute to Jeremiah's description of God as a potter who puts broken vessels back together. The name reflected his decision to focus his ministry on helping people who are broken in spirit. "My assignment is to open the door of the Church for hurting people and refocus what the Church was meant to be in our society," he said. "The Church has become stereotyped as a 'spiritual club' for elitists and yuppies who portray themselves as persons who 'have arrived.' I believe the Church was meant to be a hospital for hurting people."

The first church service Jakes held at The Potter's House drew over 2,000 people and was televised on BET stations around the country. With each passing week, the number of worshipers swelled. They were drawn partly by the service's energetic mix of music and dancing, but also by Jakes's sermons, which used Biblical lessons to discuss the challenge of leading a spiritually rewarding life in the modern world. "When T.D. Jakes opens his mouth, what comes out is liquid fire," declared a fellow evangelist. "It impacts your life with a message that doesn't stop when you walk out of there."

"My assignment is to open the door of the Church for hurting people and refocus what the Church was meant to be in our society," Jakes said. "The Church has become stereotyped as a 'spiritual club' for elitists and yuppies who portray themselves as persons who 'have arrived.' I believe the Church was meant to be a hospital for hurting people."

By the end of his first year in Dallas, Jakes had added another 7,000 members to The Potter's House. The next year, another 10,000 people joined the church. The surging popularity of his ministry enabled Jakes to branch out into a number of different areas. In addition to book writing, he established a theatrical company to produce Christian-themed plays and began recording gospel music. The Potter's House also launched a number of community outreach programs, including ambitious efforts to reach inmates in prisons around the country.

In 1999, Jakes's sermons attracted a record crowd of 87,500 at the Georgia Dome in Atlanta.

By 1999 it was clear that in the space of a few short years, Jakes had become one of the best-known evangelists in the country. That year, he preached to a record crowd of 87,500 people at the Georgia Dome in Atlanta. He was also the keynote speaker for a National Day of Prayer in Washington, D.C. In 2000 he gave the keynote addresses at annual conferences of the National Council of Black Mayors, the National Black Police Association, and the Congressional Black Caucus.

In 2001 Jakes's fame reached a new plateau when *Time* featured him in a long cover story, calling him "America's best preacher." "He is a virtuoso, a prodigy," declared David Van Biemathe in *Time*. "The only thing more exhilarating than the style of T.D. Jakes's sermons is their rigor and compassion. . . . As a preacher, Jakes takes on still-taboo topics like physical and sexual abuse and the shame of incarceration with a cathartic and psychologically acute explicitness." Around this same time, other major media outlets turned their spotlight on him as well. The *Washington Post,* for example, described him as "perhaps the greatest preaching phenomenon in black America and by some people's reckoning, all of America."

Establishing Himself as a Powerful, Prolific Writer

During Jakes's rise to stardom, he used a variety of creative avenues to express his religious faith. For example, he unveiled a theatrical version of

Woman, Thou Art Loosed!, in which a physically and emotionally abused woman struggles to build a new life for herself. That later led to a film version of the play, starring Jakes himself, which was released in 2004 to acclaim from church groups around the country. His gospel albums have been similarly successful. A 2001 gospel album called *The Storm Is Over*, featuring Jakes and the Potter House Choir, became the No. 1 gospel album in the country, and other recordings have earned Grammy and Dove Award nominations.

But book writing remained perhaps Jakes's favorite artistic means of declaring his faith and reaching out to people struggling to find happiness in the world. Since the 1993 publication of *Woman, Thou Art Loosed!* — which has sold more than 1.5 million copies — he was written more than two dozen other books. In virtually all of these works, Jakes uses his interpretations of Jesus's teaching to help guide readers to more satisfying and rewarding lives.

"When T.D. Jakes opens his mouth, what comes out is liquid fire," declared a fellow evangelist. "It impacts your life with a message that doesn't stop when you walk out of there."

In 1998, for example, Jakes published *The Lady, Her Lover, and Her Lord*, which provides instruction to women seeking positive relationships with both God and their life partners. "Here, he demonstrates an unusual ability to inspire, uplift, teach, and comfort," commented a reviewer in *Publishers Weekly*. "An eloquent wordsmith, this African-American minister writes with an abundance of memorable metaphors and yet speaks to women's hearts in practical, often humorous terms." In *The Great Investment: Faith, Family, and Finance* (2000), meanwhile, Jakes turns his attention to economic empowerment for Christians. *Publishers Weekly* praised this work as well, stating that it "quite effectively addresses nontraditional [family] configurations such as blended, one-parent, and grandmother-headed families in a supportive and non-judgmental tone."

In 2002 Jakes released another book that vaulted onto the religious bestseller list. *God's Leading Lady* combined the examples of highly successful women with personal experiences from his own life to provide readers with guidance on navigating a wide assortment of challenges. "This is a book for women of all ages and of all economic and social statuses, and it speaks to a range of issues from single motherhood to ill health to financial crises to troubled marriages," observed *Booklist*. "Jakes's fans will love this latest message of encouragement and spiritual empowerment."

Other recent books penned by Jakes include *Cover Girls* (2003), a novel of spiritual hope and inspiration, and *He-Motions: Even Strong Men Struggle* (2004), which features what *Publishers Weekly* called a "distinctly unmacho vision of fatherhood, friendship, and lifelong marital romance." In addition, Jakes contributes regular columns to national magazines like *Gospel Today, Christianity Today,* and *Ministries Today,* and he has joined with Hallmark Cards to produce a popular line of "Loose Your Spirit" inspirational greeting cards.

Promoting a Philosophy of Self-Worth

———— **"** ————

"The greatest gift you can give to a person is a resolution, so they can move on," Jakes has said. "Getting over the past has nothing to do with the person who hurt you way back when coming back to ask forgiveness. I try to help people take the past in hand and say, 'It's over, I'm moving on.'"

———— **"** ————

Both in his sermons and in his books, Jakes emphasizes his belief that unhappy people can change their lives for the better. "Too often, I'm afraid, [people] think they've identified their life story's genre and feel compelled to live it out without questioning the areas they could change," he wrote in *God's Leading Lady.* "Have you already decided you know how the story ends? What kinds of things do you allow yourself to hope for? Do you keep your hopes safe and predictable, like a familiar sitcom's ending, or do you dare believe that the impossible can happen? I believe [everyone] must harbor at least one impossible dream, an area [he or] she feels led to pursue despite the odds. It may be with [a] job, or with your broken marriage, with estranged children or with health, but I believe God wants us to expect the unexpected from Him. Too often, many people write off the end of the story before the show has ended. Leave room for Him to work in your life. . . . Hold on to your dreams, and with calm perseverance you, too, will see your promise fulfilled."

Jakes is convinced that if people can learn to put pain and suffering behind them, they can begin walking a new path of renewal and self-regard. "The greatest gift you can give to a person is a resolution, so they can move on," Jakes has said. "Getting over the past has nothing to do with the person

Jakes's ministry has been especially valuable to women.

who hurt you way back when coming back to ask forgiveness. I try to help people take the past in hand and say, 'It's over, I'm moving on.'"

Jakes believes that his ministry can be especially valuable to women. "I bring a fresh perspective to women's problems," he said. "Women have women friends to talk to, they go to women's seminars, read women's books. But their problems are with men. I tell them what men are all about." In addition, he insists that women not judge whether their lives are successful simply by the presence or absence of a romantic partner in their lives. "Your self-esteem is not tied to having a man in your life, for that's too much power to give to one person," he declared. "But when you are valuable in and of yourself and think highly of yourself, you are much more likely to draw someone who thinks highly of you as well."

Despite his immensely popular ministry, however, Jakes claims that his success is due to God. "It has more to do with God's timing and His purpose for my life than my gifts or abilities," he said. "My responsibility to the Body of Christ is almost like a spiritual physician who has discovered some medicine in the Word of God. I believe this medicine will help heal some of the hurts that are in this world. As the physician, I am careful always to acknowledge that I am not the cure, but that I have been able to facilitate the cure because Jesus Christ lives within me."

Addressing Controversy

Not surprisingly, Jakes's interpersonal skills, his oratorical abilities, and his seemingly limitless energy have drawn praise not only from his congregation, but from community activists, fellow ministers, and other observers. "He's pretty darn impressive," said Joel Fontinos, director of religious publishing at Putnam. "He draws huge crowds, sells hundreds of thousands of books, he has record deals and inner-city ministries. There's so much to him. He's so complex and multifaceted. He cuts across a lot of boundaries."

Jakes's emergence as a national figure has not been completely trouble-free, however. Some critics have complained that his ministry places too much emphasis on financial and material gain and not enough on spiritual matters. Minister Eugene Rivers, for example, charges that "[Jakes] is not offering black Christians a developed sense of biblical justice, like we got from [Martin Luther] King. The prophetic dimension of biblical faith is absent from Jakes's teaching. . . . I want to know what the end game is beyond wealth accumulation and marketing." This criticism has been sharpened by Jakes's friendships with various celebrities and sports stars, as well as by the minister's lifestyle. He lives with his family in a huge mansion, selects luxurious accommodations wherever he travels, and displays very expensive taste in suits and jewelry.

Jakes rejects claims that he dwells too much on economic matters, though. "[I have to] talk about economic empowerment because it is a reality for my people," he stated. "The only solution to our generation, particularly in the inner cities where there are racial issues and academic issues and people are on their second and third chances, is [to teach economic empowerment]. . . . If we don't teach economic empowerment, we will subtly create atmospheres that promote crime and drugs and pestilence in our community. I'm not evaluating the integrity of your faith by the depth of your wallet."

In addition, Jakes makes no apologies for his lifestyle. "I see no need to hide the fact that God has blessed me as a business person, investor, and author," he wrote on his web site. "Any time Christians become very, very successful, others attempt to discredit us. . . . In a time when we're saying to African-American men — and men in general — to take care of their children, we ought to celebrate any man who has found financial security and is also a minister. I don't see that as a minus." In fact, Jakes told the *Washington Post* that he sees his success as an inspiration to others. "Once [young African Americans] see a black man who is successful, who has written several books and been celebrated [across] the country and overseas, and he's not selling drugs but he's driving the same kind of car the pimp or drug dealer is, and he's not illegal and he's not immoral, it encourages young men. . . . They say, 'Hey, if God can do it for him, he can do it for me, too.'"

Some Pentecostal religious leaders have also questioned aspects of Jakes's theological beliefs — specifically his continued affiliation with the Higher Ground Always Abounding Assemblies. Churches in this organization follow a doctrine commonly called "Oneness Pentecostalism," a belief that Jesus Christ alone is God. Other Pentecostal denominations, however, embrace the traditional Christian concept of a Holy Trinity consisting of the Father, Son, and Holy Spirit.

When criticism of Jakes in this area was publicized in *Christianity Today* in 2000, the leader of The Potter's House responded quickly. "My association with Oneness people does not constitute assimilation into their ranks any more than my association with the homeless in our city makes me one of them," he wrote in a response published in the same magazine.

———— **"** ————

"I see no need to hide the fact that God has blessed me as a business person, investor, and author," he wrote on his web site. *"Any time Christians become very, very successful, others attempt to discredit us. . . . In a time when we're saying to African-American men — and men in general — to take care of their children, we ought to celebrate any man who has found financial security and is also a minister. I don't see that as a minus."*

———— **"** ————

"While I mix with Christians from a broad range of theological perspectives, I speak only for my personal faith and convictions. . . . I believe in one God who is the Father, the Son, and the Holy Spirit. I believe these three have distinct and separate functions — so separate that each has individual attributes, yet are one. I do not believe in three Gods. . . . When I think of the Trinity, I consider how Jesus prayed under the unction of the Holy Spirit that we would be one even as He and the Father are one. To that end, I preach, write, and work."

The Potter's House has grown into a multiracial, nondenominational church with more than 28,000 members.

Building an Empire

Today, Jakes leads a religious empire of truly amazing size and scope. The Potter's House has grown into a multiracial, nondenominational church with 59 active internal and outreach ministries and more than 28,000 members. The church facility is also one of the largest and most technologically modern in the country. In addition to seating capacity for 8,200 (Sunday attendance is spread over three services), the church features a concert-quality sound system and laptop terminals that enable worshipers to download sermon notes and other information directly from their pews. The weekly services from The Potter's House appear on the Trinity Broadcasting Network (TBN), Black Entertainment Television (BET), the Daystar Network, and an assortment of foreign networks. In addition, Jakes has developed "The Potter's Touch," a daily 30-minute talk show focusing on religious and self-help issues that appears on both TBN and BET.

Jakes is particularly proud of the church's outreach programs, which target virtually every needy demographic group in America. Programs include the Guardians, which reaches out to homeless people; Rahab International, which helps prostitutes and women in abusive domestic situations; a Transformation Treatment Program for drug and alcohol abusers; an AIDS outreach initiative; a Fire House youth ministry; and the Prison Satellite Network, which provides gospel programming to more than 350,000 inmates in 375 prisons in 40 states. "Most of our Bible was written in prison, by inmates," Jakes explained on his official web site. "Some of the greatest men that God ever used were incarcerated. In fact Jesus himself was incarcerated, locked up and executed. Jeremiah, Joseph, Peter, and the Apostle Paul were incarcerated. Many of the great people of faith, received their faith in prison—and were able to make a significant contribution to the world."

Other notable institutions established by Jakes and The Potter's House include Clay Academy, a private Christian preparatory school for children from kindergarten through eighth grade, and the Metroplex Economic Development Corporation (MEDC), a nonprofit organization. The MEDC was founded to "transform urban America by creating a platform for social and economic awareness," according to The Potter's House Web site. The corporation's activities include employment services, business development, political outreach, and strategic partnerships with corporate and civic organizations. Jakes also serves as Chief Executive Officer (CEO) of The Potter's House Ministries, a nonprofit organization that each year produces several major national conferences for Christian men, women, and youth.

"I'm certainly a Type-A, high-energy person," Jakes observed. "There's never enough time in the day to do everything that I want to do. I finally realized I'm the kind of person who enjoys being busy. When I'm overwhelmed, I back away. Get some rest and then go back and do it again. . . . I feel as though my area of expertise is to work with people who are emotionally hurt or wounded and to watch them recover. And to see them restored."

In addition to all his evangelical and community oriented work, Jakes directs the for-profit company T.D. Jakes Enterprises. Many of Jakes's books, videotapes, and audiotapes of various sermons and speeches are made available through this company. Other resources managed by T.D. Jakes Enterprises include Touchdown Concepts, his theatrical production company; and Dexterity Sounds, his gospel music label.

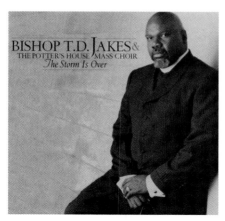

Jakes's 2001 gospel CD The Storm Is Over *became the No. 1 gospel album in the country.*

Jakes admits that it is a challenge to stay on top of his many responsibilities. "My struggle is the scheduling, stress, busyness, weariness —the loss of normalcy and privacy," he said. "Sometimes the crowds are overwhelming. Those kinds of things are perplexing for a country boy from West Virginia." But he notes that he only needs about four hours of sleep a night. "I'm certainly a Type-A, high-energy person," he observed. "There's never enough time in the day to do everything that I want to do. I finally realized I'm the kind of person who enjoys being busy. When I'm overwhelmed, I back away. Get some rest and then go back and do it again. . . . I feel as though my area of expertise is to work with people who are emotionally hurt or wounded and to watch them recover. And to see them restored."

MARRIAGE AND FAMILY

Jakes married Serita A. Jamison in 1981. They have three sons, Jamar, Jermaine, and T. Dexter, Jr.; and two daughters, Cora and Sarah. Jakes commonly tells people that he could never have built his successful ministry without the support of his wife, a fellow author who helps direct various Potter's House programs. "She's the butter in my biscuit, she's the gravy on my grits," declared Jakes. "She's essential to the running of this place."

HOBBIES AND OTHER INTERESTS

Jakes's many evangelical, community, and entrepreneurial activities leave him little time for hobbies. He has said, however, that "my idea of having a good time is sitting around with the kids acting crazy. You know, stuff you could do if you was broke."

SELECTED WORKS

Writings

Woman Thou Art Loosed!, 1993
Can You Stand to Be Blessed?, 1995

Help Me, I've Fallen, 1995
The Harvest, 1995
Naked and Not Ashamed, 1995
Loose That Man and Let Him Go!, 1996
Daddy Loves His Girls, 1996
Water in the Wilderness, 1996
Why? Because You Are Anointed, 1996
T.D. Jakes Speaks to Women!, 1996
Help! I'm Raising My Child Alone, 1996
A Fresh Glimpse of the Dove, 1997
When Shepherds Bleed, 1997
T.D. Jakes Speaks to Men!, 1997
I Choose to Forgive, 1997
So You Call Yourself a Man?, 1997
Lay Aside the Weight, 1997
The Lady, Her Lover, and Her Lord, 1998
His Lady, 1999
Maximize the Moment, 2000
The Great Investment, 2001
God's Leading Lady, 2002
He-Motions, 2004

Recordings

Live at The Potter's House, 1999
The Storm Is Over, 2002
Follow the Star, 2003
A Wing and a Prayer, 2004

HONORS AND AWARDS

Gospel Heritage Award for Ministry (*Gospel Today* magazine): 1999
Living Legend Award (National Professional Network): 2000
Chairman's Award (National Religious Broadcasters): 2002
NAACP Image Award: 2002, for *The Storm Is Over*

FURTHER READING

Books

Contemporary Black Biography, Vol. 17, 1998; Vol. 43, 2004
Hinds, Patricia M., ed. *50 of the Most Inspiring African Americans,* 2002
Religious Leaders of America, 1999

Wellman, Sam. *T.D. Jakes,* 2000
Who's Who among African Americans, 2003

Periodicals

Baltimore Sun, Aug. 24, 1998, p.E5
Boston Globe, Oct. 21, 2004, p.D1
Christianity Today, Feb. 7, 2000, p.52; Feb. 21, 2000
Cleveland Plain Dealer, Sep. 22, 2000, p.E1
Current Biography Yearbook, 2001
Dallas Morning News, Jan. 24, 1999, p.E1
Detroit News, Oct. 16, 2004, p.D1
Ebony, Oct. 1998, p.92; Jan. 2001, p.108; Oct. 2002, p.24
Essence, Dec. 2001, p.126; Feb. 2003, p.210; Aug. 2003, p.116
Houston Chronicle, July 12, 2003, p.1
Jet, Dec. 22, 2003, p.57
Los Angeles Times, Aug. 20, 1998, p.E1
New York Times, Jan. 1, 1999, p.A1
People, Nov. 9, 1998, p.121
Time, Sep. 17, 2001, p.52
USA Today, Dec. 27, 2000, p.D8
Wall Street Journal, Aug. 21, 1998, p.A1
Washington Post, Sep. 11, 1999, p.B1; Mar. 25, 2001, p.S1

Online Databases

Biography Resource Center Online, 2004, articles from *Contemporary Authors Online,* 2004; *Contemporary Black Biography,* 2004; *Religious Leaders of America,* 1999; and *Who's Who among African Americans,* 2004

ADDRESS

T.D. Jakes
The Potter's House
6777 West Kiest Blvd.
Dallas, TX 75236

WORLD WIDE WEB SITES

http://www.tdjakes.org
http://www.thepottershouse.org
http://www.thepotterstouch.org

Toby Keith 1961-

American Country Music Singer, Songwriter,
and Guitarist
Two-Time Winner of the Entertainer of the Year
Award from the Academy of Country Music

BIRTH

Toby Keith was born Toby Keith Covel on July 8, 1961, in Clinton, Oklahoma. His mother, Joan Covel, was a homemaker who loved to sing. His father, Hubert K. Covel, was an oil company executive. Keith is the oldest of three children in his family. He has a younger brother, Tracy, and a younger sister, Tonni.

YOUTH

Toby Keith spent most of his childhood on the family farm in Moore, a town on the outskirts of Oklahoma City. He believes that he got his singing talent from his mother and his songwriting abilities from his father. Hubert Covel, a Korean War veteran, also taught his children to be patriotic. "He was like John Wayne," Keith recalled. "He lost his eye in a jeep accident. Went through the windshield. I was 16 or 17 before I knew that discolored eye was blind." Keith grew up sharing his father's strong loyalty to the United States, a characteristic that surfaces repeatedly in his songs.

With the support of his family, Keith started playing guitar when he was eight years old. His first instrument was a Christmas present from his maternal grandmother. His paternal grandfather, who played music in church, taught Keith his first guitar chords. Keith soon began attending jam sessions with some older boys who lived nearby. He became inspired to write his own songs, and sometimes he composed up to nine in a day. Although he admitted that these songs were not very good, he was proud that he finished every one he started.

Keith's first significant musical influences were the country musicians who performed at a supper club his grandmother owned. Keith worked in the kitchen of the restaurant as a teenager, and the band would let him join them on stage when he finished working. This early exposure to country music helped hone his songwriting style.

Another early influence was his father's record collection. Keith listened to the legendary country singer-songwriter Merle Haggard, whom he would later cite as his main influence. He also discovered country star Willie Nelson, with whom he would later record a hit song. Other artists, including rock musicians like the Eagles and Bob Seger, inspired him as well.

EDUCATION AND FIRST JOBS

Keith received his education in the public schools in Moore. While attending Moore High School, Keith worked summers as a rodeo hand, test-riding bulls and broncos. In addition, he organized a number of his fellow music-loving rodeo hands into a country-rock band called Easy Money, which performed at local bars on weekends.

Because of his imposing physical size, Keith was sometimes called upon to break up barroom fights during his early musical career. "The places I first played in, if a fight broke out, it could clear the bar," he remembered. "They couldn't afford bouncers [security people], so I'd have to do something to keep from losing my audience. If I saw a big fight fixing to happen, I'd put down my guitar and jump off the stage. I'm 6-foot-4, 235 pounds, plus I'd be sober and the other guys were drunk. That's a great advantage."

After graduating from high school in the late 1970s, Keith worked with his father in the local oil fields. He started out as a low-level laborer and worked his way up to operational manager over the next few years. Eventually he traded the oil fields for the football field and played defensive end for the Oklahoma City Drillers, a semi-professional football team. In 1984 Keith tried out for the Oklahoma Outlaws—a professional franchise in the now-defunct United States Football League (USFL)—but failed to make the team.

Easy Money was "up against the best bands in the world," Keith acknowledged. "The competition's fierce, and if you can make it there, you can make it anywhere. I'm not bragging when I say that the Easy Money Band and I can hold our own against any of them."

CAREER HIGHLIGHTS

Throughout his years working in the oil industry and playing football, Keith continued playing with his band, Easy Money. After his unsuccessful tryout with the Outlaws football team, he decided to focus on music. His band went on tour, playing at clubs in Oklahoma, Texas, and Louisiana. Meanwhile, Keith sent demo tapes of his own music to record companies in Nashville, Tennessee—the country music capital of the United States. None of the record companies expressed any interest at first, but Keith refused to abandon his dream of a big music career.

This grit and determination eventually paid off. Toby Keith and Easy Money gained momentum throughout the mid-1980s. By 1988 they had moved beyond the Texas and Oklahoma club circuits and were playing at bigger, more profitable venues throughout the western United States. Hopeful that they were on the verge of national success, Keith even purchased a tour bus for the band. Easy Money was "up against the best bands in the world," he acknowledged. "The competition's fierce, and if you can make it

there, you can make it anywhere. I'm not bragging when I say that the Easy Money Band and I can hold our own against any of them."

Signing His First Recording Contract

Easy Money had been together almost 10 years when its leader finally got his big break. While in Nashville, Keith gave a demo tape to Harold Shedd, the president of Mercury Records. He was shocked when Shedd called him a few days later and offered to fly out to one of his Oklahoma City shows. Shedd signed Keith to a record deal over breakfast on the day after the concert.

Keith released his first album, entitled *Toby Keith,* in 1993. It was a remarkably successful debut effort, producing three No. 1 hits. The first single, "Should've Been a Cowboy," topped the *Billboard* magazine country singles chart, followed by "Wish I Didn't Know Now" and "A Little Less Talk and a Lot More Action." Another song, "He Ain't Worth Missing," reached the No. 5 spot. *Toby Keith* eventually sold more than two million copies, earning "double platinum" status.

Shedd soon left Mercury and joined Polydor Records. Eager to continue their working relationship, Keith followed him and signed a new deal with Polydor. He released his second album, *Boomtown*, in 1994. Although it was not quite as successful as his debut effort, it sold more than 500,000 copies. It also produced a No. 1 hit single, "Who's That Man," and a Top 5 hit, "You Ain't Much Fun."

The songs on Keith's first two albums cemented his reputation as a working-man's poet. The title track on *Boom-town*, for example, tells the story of an oil town that experiences a fleeting boom and then goes bankrupt. "I lived that song, watched it happen in Elk Town, Oklahoma," Keith explained. "Elk Town went from being Small Town USA to Boomtown overnight, as they brought in 1,500 oil rigs and started pumping. For six years, you had corporate people coming in from Houston and Saudi Arabia. . . . Everybody had money, even people who were living under overpasses, because there wasn't enough housing for everybody." Then the oil industry went into a slump, with disastrous results for the town. "The wells ran dry," Keith recalled. "The rich people got rich by saving their money. The fools who got it and spent it were broke."

> *"I lived that song, watched it happen in Elk Town, Oklahoma," Keith said about "Boomtown." "Elk Town went from being Small Town USA to Boomtown overnight, as they brought in 1,500 oil rigs and started pumping. . . . Everybody had money, even people who were living under overpasses, because there wasn't enough housing for everybody. . . . [Then] the wells ran dry. The rich people got rich by saving their money. The fools who got it and spent it were broke."*

Keith released his next record, a collection of 12 holiday songs called *Christmas to Christmas*, in 1995. "It doesn't have any traditional Christmas songs on it," he noted. "Instead of this just being a Christmas album, I wanted this to be an album like I usually do, but with a Christmas theme. This sounds like anything else of mine that you would hear on the radio. It just happens to be about Christmas." Keith's fourth record, *Blue Moon*, was

83

Keith and Sting performed their hit song "I'm So Happy I Can't Stop Crying" at the 1997 Country Music Association Awards.

released in 1996 and went platinum, meaning that it sold over a million copies.

Around this time Polydor ceased operations in Nashville. Keith then returned to Mercury, which maintained offices in the country music capital. He released his next record, *Dream Walkin'*, on the Mercury label in 1997. It featured two songs that reached the No. 2 spot on the *Billboard* country charts: the ballad "When We Were in Love," and a duet with the rock musician Sting called "I'm So Happy I Can't Stop Crying." This song, which Sting composed, was nominated for a Grammy Award — one of the most coveted awards in the music industry. Sting joined Keith on television later that year to perform the song on the Country Music Association's awards show.

Breaking Through to a Wider Audience

In 1998 Keith released his *Greatest Hits, Volume I*. By this time, he was regarded as one of the rising stars of country music, but he had not yet broken through to attract a mainstream audience. He placed part of the blame on Mercury, which he felt had not done a satisfactory job of promoting his records. After the release of his *Greatest Hits* album, Keith left Mercury and signed with a new label, DreamWorks Nashville.

His next album proved to be a breakthrough effort. *How Do You Like Me Now?!*, released in 1999, marked Keith's first collaboration with Dream-Works and producer James Stroud. It featured two No. 1 hits. The song "How Do You Like Me Now?" sat at the top of the country charts for five weeks and became Keith's first Top 40 hit on the pop charts. The next hit single, "You Shouldn't Kiss Me Like This," remained at No. 1 on the country charts for three weeks.

How Do You Like Me Now?! eventually sold more than one million copies and brought Keith several long-awaited award nominations. He claimed two prestigious honors at the 2000 Academy of Country Music Awards: Male Vocalist of the Year and Album of the Year.

That success was repeated on Keith's 2001 album, *Pull My Chain,* which produced three No. 1 singles and a slew of award nominations. Two songs from the album, "My List" and "I Wanna Talk About Me," each spent five weeks at the top of the charts. The Country Music Association honored Keith as the year's best male vocalist.

"I'm stalking him," stated Warren Littlefield, former president of the NBC network, about his efforts to sign up Keith for a TV sitcom. "He's a personality, he's a performer, and he's funny. Last time I checked, that's what makes for great television."

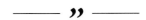

As Keith's music began to achieve crossover success, the singer received several opportunities to try his hand at acting. He made brief television appearances in the series "Touched by an Angel" and in the "Dukes of Hazzard" reunion movie. He also starred in television commercials for Ford Trucks, Mr. Coffee, and other products.

Television executives noticed Keith's screen presence and approached him to star in a situation comedy series. "I'm stalking him," stated Warren Littlefield, former president of the NBC network. "He's a personality, he's a performer, and he's funny. Last time I checked, that's what makes for great television." Keith admitted that he was tempted by the offer to star in his own TV show, but he decided that it would take too much time away from his music. "I just can't do that," he said.

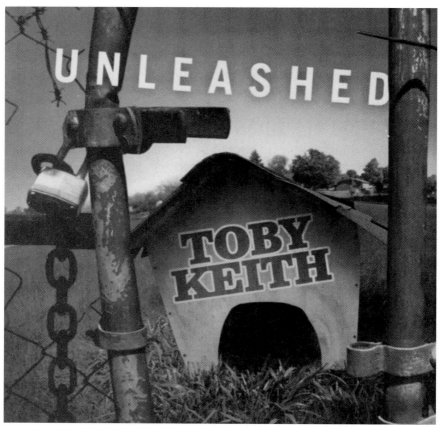

The emotionally volatile song "Courtesy of the Red, White, and Blue
(The Angry American)" appeared on Keith's CD Unleashed.

Responding to the September 11 Tragedy

Despite his growing personal success, the year 2001 was tragic for Keith, as it was for all Americans. On March 24 his father died of a heart attack while driving. Six months later, the entire nation reeled from the September 11 terrorist attacks on the World Trade Center in New York City and the Pentagon in Washington, D.C., along with the plane crash in Pennsylvania.

The loss of his father, coupled with the events of 9/11, inspired Keith to write what is probably his best-known song: "Courtesy of the Red, White, and Blue (The Angry American)." Its emotionally charged lyrics denounce terrorist groups: The song condemns Al Qaeda, the terrorist organization that orchestrated the attacks, and the Taliban, the radical Islamic government of Afghanistan that sheltered terrorist leader Osama bin Laden. The song also pays tribute to Hubert Covel and the patriotism he instilled in his children. "I really wanted it as an honor and a tribute to my dad," Keith explained. "I wanted to go out and sing it to military people."

"Courtesy of the Red, White, and Blue" appeared on Keith's 2002 album, *Unleashed*. Keith originally had not planned to record the song. But after he performed it at a military event in Washington, D.C., a general in attendance told him that it was his "responsibility" to record it. It later proved extremely popular with the U.S. troops that took part in the 2003 invasion of the Middle Eastern nation of Iraq. "Courtesy of the Red, White, and Blue" became a sort of anthem for the American forces during the Iraq War. Many soldiers painted the song's title on bombs and tanks. One soldier, Private First Class Patrick Miller, told reporters that after he was taken prisoner by Iraqi forces in an ambush, he sang it to his captors "just to make 'em mad."

After September 11, "Courtesy of the Red, White, and Blue" generated strong responses from listeners, both positive and negative. "The response was so tremendous," Keith stated. "I know how angry I was when those towers came down, and this is my way of serving my country."

Creating Controversy

From the beginning, the song generated strong responses from listeners, both positive and negative. Many people, furious over the 9/11 attacks, applauded its angry call for revenge and unabashed patriotism. "The response was so tremendous," Keith stated. "I know how angry I was when those towers came down, and this is my way of serving my country." Other listeners, though, condemned the song as overly aggressive.

An ABC television special stirred up additional controversy about the song. The network invited Keith to sing it on "In Search of America: A July Fourth Musical Celebration." A short time later, Peter Jennings, the show's host, convinced ABC to rescind its invitation. Jennings felt that the song's lyrics were inappropriate for the show. Keith's fans were outraged by the network's decision. They swamped ABC with calls, letters, and e-mails in protest, but Keith remained off of the guest list.

Keith soon found himself at the center of another flap. Natalie Maines, lead singer of the all-female country group the Dixie Chicks, gave an interview in which she harshly criticized "Courtesy of the Red, White, and Blue." "I hate it," Maines stated. "It's ignorant, and it makes country music sound ignorant." Keith reacted to this criticism by saying, "You've got to be in my league as a songwriter before I'll even respond to you." The ABC incident, Maines's comments, and Keith's response made him the center of a great deal of media attention. The publicity actually worked in his favor, however, because it shined a spotlight on the song and album. Partly as a result, *Unleashed* debuted as the best-selling album on both the pop and country charts in July 2002. It eventually sold three million copies and was certified triple platinum.

Although "Courtesy of the Red, White, and Blue" generated the strongest response, others songs on the record proved immensely popular as well. "Who's Your Daddy?" and "Beer for My Horses" both became hits. "Beer for My Horses" is a duet that Keith recorded with his longtime idol Willie Nelson. The two men performed the song at the Farm Aid benefit concert in Pittsburgh in 2002. The lyrics talk about justice and the way it was served in the Old West. Although the song was written before September 11, its harsh sentiments struck a chord with many people outraged by the terrorist attacks.

Keith and Nelson reunited to perform the song at the Academy of Country Music's 2002 awards show. The Dixie Chicks were unable to attend and arranged instead to be broadcast live on a television screen at the ceremony. Maines appeared wearing a T-shirt with an insulting slogan and Keith's initials on it. When Keith failed to show up a short time later to accept the "Entertainer of the Year" award, some believed that he had left the theater in anger. But he later said that he had retired to his tour bus to write a song with Nelson.

Speaking for Soldiers and Hard-Working Americans

Keith followed up on the success of *Unleashed* with *Shock'n Y'all,* which debuted at number one upon its release in 2003. Like most of his records, the album was tinged with patriotic sentiments. It also demonstrated Keith's sense of humor. "We were looking for album titles while the war was going on," he explained. "Then the 'Shock and Awe' [military] campaign started, and it became such a funny phrase; I thought it would be funny to take that, add a 'y'all' on the end and throw a little hillbilly at 'em."

Keith recorded *Shock'n Y'all* at the Shrimp Boat Sound Studio in Key West, Florida, the recording facility owned by singer-songwriter Jimmy Buffett. While he was making the album, Keith was called away by the president of the United States. President George W. Bush invited Keith to attend a

Along with President George W. Bush, Keith visited soldiers at
MacDill Air Force Base in Florida.

speech he was giving to General Tommy Franks and his troops at MacDill Air Force Base in Tampa. The singer proudly accepted, and he treated soldiers and their families to a brief performance, using only an acoustic guitar.

Shock'n Y'all added to Keith's reputation as a songwriter who speaks to the concerns of American soldiers and other hard-working people. The song "American Soldier," for example, tries to see the world through the eyes of a U.S. enlisted man stationed in Iraq. Keith continued to express his patriotism and his support for American troops. "I'm not for every war, and I'm not against every war," he noted, "and I don't consider myself smart enough to say whether or not we should be [in Iraq]. This is just my way of letting everybody know exactly what a soldier is: just another American that gets up and goes to work."

In 2004 Keith released his *Greatest Hits, Volume 2* album, featuring favorite songs recorded before *Shock 'n Y'all*. He continues to tour constantly and perform at awards shows and other high-profile venues. He headlined a nationally televised pre-kickoff concert at the 2004 Super Bowl, for example, and he took the stage again at halftime to perform "Walk This Way" and "Sweet Emotion" with the rock group Aerosmith.

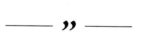

> "*I'm not for every war, and I'm not against every war," Keith noted, "and I don't consider myself smart enough to say whether or not we should be [in Iraq]. This is just my way of letting everybody know exactly what a soldier is: just another American that gets up and goes to work.*"

Over the course of his 20-year career, Toby Keith has gone from breaking up fights in small clubs to headlining concerts in sold-out stadiums. Despite his success, however, he has never lost track of his roots. In fact, he claims that being in big cities like New York only makes him yearn for the country. "After three days, I've got to find some grass," he stated. "You can go to Central Park, but that's just a quick fix. I've got to be able to see grass way off in the distance. I'm always going to be a country boy."

MARRIAGE AND FAMILY

When he is not traveling with his band, Keith loves to spend time with his family. He met his wife, Tricia Lucus Covel, at a club where he was playing with Easy Money. "I was 19, and he was 20," she recalled. "He was just one of those larger-than-life guys, full of confidence." They dated for three years before marrying in 1984. Keith has two daughters, Shelley and Krystal, and one son, Stelen. The family makes their home on a 160-acre ranch near Norman, Oklahoma, called Dream Walkin' Farms, where Keith raises and trains about 50 racehorses.

HOBBIES AND OTHER INTERESTS

Keith has always loved sports. He works out at the gym, runs, and is an avid golfer. He is a devoted fan of the University of Oklahoma Sooners basketball and football teams. Both of his daughters attend Oklahoma, and he frequently makes financial donations to the university.

The singer also does charity work. In 2003 he organized the "Toby Keith and Friends Golf Classic," which raised an estimated $250,000 for "Ally's House," a nonprofit organization that assists the families of pediatric cancer patients. The foundation takes its name from Ally Webb, the daughter of Keith's former band mate, Scott Webb. Ally died of liver cancer at the age of two.

In 1999 an elementary school in Keith's hometown of Moore was flattened by a tornado. The country music star responded by holding a benefit concert to raise money to rebuild the school. In December 2000 the students planted a tree in Keith's honor.

Keith is also becoming involved in various business interests. He purchased the Belmar Golf Club in Norman in 2004. He also purchased a 12,000-square-foot piece of property that will one day be home to "Toby Keith's Road House," a $4.5 million restaurant and music hall.

RECORDINGS

Toby Keith, 1993
Boomtown, 1994
Christmas to Christmas, 1995
Blue Moon, 1996
Dream Walkin', 1997
Greatest Hits, Volume I, 1998
How Do You Like Me Now?!, 1999
Pull My Chain, 2001
Unleashed, 2002
Shock'n Y'all, 2003
Greatest Hits, Volume 2, 2004

HONORS AND AWARDS

Male Video Artist of the Year (Country Music Television): 2000
Video of the Year (Country Music Television): 2000, for "How Do You Like
   Me Now?!"
Male Vocalist of the Year (Academy of Country Music): 2001, 2004
Entertainer of the Year (Academy of Country Music): 2003, 2004
Favorite Country Album (American Music Awards): 2003, for *Unleashed*
Flameworthy Male Video of the Year and Cocky Video of the Year (Country
   Music Television): 2003, for "Courtesy of the Red, White, and Blue"
People's Choice Award: 2004, for *Unleashed,* for Favorite Album
Album of the Year (Academy of Country Music): 2004, for *Shock'n Y'All*
Video of the Year (Academy of Country Music): 2004, for "Beer for My
   Horses"
Flameworthy Video of the Year (Country Music Television): 2004, for
   "American Soldier"
Flameworthy Video Collaboration of the Year (Country Music Television):
   2004, for "Beer for My Horses" with Willie Nelson

FURTHER READING

Books

Contemporary Musicians, Vol. 40, 2003

Periodicals

Airplay Monitor, Oct. 24, 2003, p.31
Arizona Daily Star, Sep. 27, 2002, p.F4
Baltimore Sun, Nov. 19, 2002, p.E1
Boston Globe, July 23, 2004, p.C1

Daily Oklahoman, May 25, 2004, p.A1
Entertainment Weekly, Oct. 31, 2003, p.38
GQ, Jan. 2004, p.46
Minneapolis Star Tribune, Feb. 28, 2003, p.E1
National Catholic Reporter, Sep. 6, 2002, p.12
People, June 25, 2001, p.71
Phoenix New Times, Sep. 26, 2002
Rolling Stone, Jan. 22, 2004, p.43
Sunday Oklahoman, Aug. 22, 2004, p.C1
Time, Mar. 1, 2004, p.75
USA Weekend, Aug. 20, 2000; Nov. 2, 2003, p.6

Online Articles

http://launch.yahoo.com
  (Launch Music, "Toby Keith: The Sting of Success," Aug. 28, 1997)
http://www.usaweekend.com
  (*USA Weekend*, "An Outsider and Proud of It," Aug. 20, 2000; "Red,
  White, and Cowboy Blues," Nov. 2, 2004)
http://www.usatoday.com
  (*USA Today*, "Singer Toby Keith Speaks Out on ABC Censorship," June
  13, 2002)

Online Databases

Biography Resource Center Online, 2004, article from *Contemporary
Musicians*, 2003

ADDRESS

Toby Keith
TKO Artist Management
1107 17th Avenue
South Nashville, TN 37212

WORLD WIDE WEB SITES

http://www.tobykeith.com
http://www.tobykeith.dreamworksnashville.com
http://www.allmusic.com
http://www.cmt.com/artists

Karen Mitchell-Raptakis 1956-

American Greeting Card Entrepreneur
Creator of the "It's a Sista Thing!"™ Line of
Greeting Cards

BIRTH

Karen Mitchell-Raptakis was born Karen Mitchell on August
14, 1956, in Brooklyn, a borough of New York City. Her father,
Desburnie Mitchell, was a postman and part-time TV repair-
man. Her mother, Frances Mitchell, was a customer service rep
at Macy's department store and later worked for the city of
New York in the Marriage License bureau. Karen has one sis-

ter, Patricia, who is two years younger. In 1969, when Mitchell-Raptakis was 13, the family moved from the projects to a house in Bedford-Stuyvesant, Brooklyn.

YOUTH

Mitchell-Raptakis was raised in the housing projects of Brownsville, Brooklyn. As a child, she enjoyed spending time on creative activities indoors, like reading, writing, and art projects. She loved to draw women's clothing and fashion and to paint the paint-by-number kits that her father occasionally brought her. "Although I enjoyed playing outside with my friends, I actually preferred to stay in my room so I could write, read, or draw," she recalls. "I always carried a book with me. My parents loved reading and passed that love on to my sister and I. But Mama and Daddy didn't understand why their oldest daughter liked to write so much. They wanted me to go outside more. 'I'd rather write,' I'd tell them."

Mitchell-Raptakis remembers making her first greeting card for her mother when she was in kindergarten. She always loved greeting cards. For many years she created elaborate handmade cards featuring original poems, drawings, and collages. They were very popular among her friends and relatives, who always looked forward to receiving them.

"Although I enjoyed playing outside with my friends, I actually preferred to stay in my room so I could write, read, or draw," Mitchell-Raptakis recalls. "I always carried a book with me. My parents loved reading and passed that love on to my sister and I. But Mama and Daddy didn't understand why their oldest daughter liked to write so much. They wanted me to go outside more. 'I'd rather write,' I'd tell them."

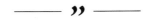

Mitchell-Raptakis grew up during the turbulent 1960s. Black people in the South were denied the right to vote and prevented from attending the same schools as white people. Apartheid, the separation of the races, was the law in South Africa. War was raging in Vietnam. And young Karen was being bussed to an all-white school. Legally, schools had been required to integrate during the 1950s. But in fact many schools around the country were still segregated by race. To change that, school districts tried bussing students from one school district to the next. Karen and her sister were

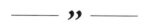

"The difference I felt from my peers forced me into a sensitive, creative shell," Mitchell-Raptakis explains. *"I was extremely shy around my classmates and teachers. I rarely raised my hand in school, even when I knew the answer. Writing sustained me as much as breathing. I found my voice while writing."*

bussed to integrated schools in white neighborhoods because her parents believed their children would get a better education there. "The difference I felt from my peers forced me into a sensitive, creative shell," she explains. "I was extremely shy around my classmates and teachers. I rarely raised my hand in school, even when I knew the answer. Writing sustained me as much as breathing. I found my voice while writing."

EDUCATION

Mitchell-Raptakis attended Samuel J. Tilden High School in Brooklyn, New York, graduating in 1974. "Writing helped me define my teenage years, when I continued to be the quiet, skinny girl with the glasses, too shy to raise her hand," she recalls. Her favorite classes in high school were art and creative writing. But she viewed these activities as enjoyable pastimes, not steps to a career. When her creative writing teacher wrote on one of her stories "I look forward to reading your books someday," that did not seem possible to Mitchell-Raptakis. She came from a hardworking and practical family, and that meant having a practical job.

From 1977 to 1981 Mitchell-Raptakis attended evening classes at the Fashion Institute of Technology in New York City and majored in advertising design. She learned how to design the old-fashioned way—without a computer—by using T-squares, rulers, x-acto knives, and rubber cement. She learned about the components of good design, typography, color theory, the history of art, and photography. She loved visiting art stores and enjoyed working with her professors, who encouraged students to try something different to stimulate their creativity. So Mitchell-Raptakis bought some pens and a book and taught herself calligraphy. In the mid-1980s she took courses at Parsons School of Design in New York City to perfect her calligraphy skills.

FIRST JOBS

Seeking independence, Mitchell-Raptakis decided to get a job right after high school. Her first permanent job was at Merrill Lynch, a brokerage firm, where she worked from 1975 to 1980 in a variety of administrative positions. From 1980 to 1984 Mitchell-Raptakis worked at another Wall Street firm as the supervisor in the Retirement Planning Department and became a licensed stockbroker. But working in the financial district did not stimulate her creatively. Something was missing. She started making collage-type greeting cards for her family by cutting and pasting ribbons, doilies, dried flowers, and other items on card stock. She also began to sell her hand-made cards and hand-painted T-shirts, hats, and denim jackets at neighborhood craft shows in Brooklyn. In 1982 she started The LDC Design Co. (Let's Design Cards) to do freelance calligraphy work, graphic design, and handmade cards.

By 1984 Mitchell-Raptakis was eager to work in a more creative environment, so she left Wall Street to work in the business office of a small advertising agency/public relations firm on Madison Avenue. After a short stay at another small ad agency, Mitchell-Raptakis was laid off because of a downturn in business. She eventually found a new position at Rockshots, a small photographic greeting card company, where she was hired as a receptionist. The owners were two men who started the business in their kitchen and expanded to a loft with warehouse space and several employees. It didn't matter that she was the receptionist—Karen was thankful for getting on-the-job training in the industry of her dreams. "Every job I've had has always been a training ground for me to learn something and reach new personal goals," she explains.

Mitchell-Raptakis gained valuable experience at Rockshots. She took orders over the phone, sat in on staff meetings to discuss new card ideas, interacted with photographers, models, and artists, and took orders at the National Stationery Show, an annual event where large and small manufacturers showcase their products. The National Stationery Show was vibrant and innovative and full of new ideas—heaven for a person who loved stationery and paper as much as Karen did.

In 1986, Mitchell-Raptakis went to work in publishing as the assistant to the vice-president of pro-

Do you remember...
8 track tapes?
The Bump?
Hot Pants?
Platform shoes?
Afro puffs?

duction. In 1998, she became the first digital archivist at the company, and she continued to work there as the digital archivist manager until 2003. As such, she ensured that digital copies of her company's books were stored in an electronic archive; she also ensured that all subsequent corrections to the printed books were maintained in the archived versions as well.

CAREER HIGHLIGHTS

Mitchell-Raptakis is the founder of The LDC Design Co., later renamed Karen & Company Greeting Cards. Her business is best known for producing a line of greeting cards called "It's a Sista Thing!"™ Aimed at African Americans, the award-winning cards celebrate the black experience and feature messages that resonate in the black community.

Developing the Idea

Mitchell-Raptakis first got the idea for her company in the early 1990s when she went shopping for a greeting card for her best friend, who was going through a crisis. She wanted a card that would offer encouragement to her friend as well as reflect the African-American heritage they shared. She wanted the card's images and words to look and sound natural, like real black women. There were no cards on the market that fit those specifications, and Mitchell-Raptakis started to think seriously about designing a line of greeting cards for African-American women. "I had a girlfriend who was going through a crisis and I wanted to send her a card, but there was nothing that said what I wanted to say to her," she recalls. "The selection of cards either had syrupy-sweet, unnatural-sounding messages, or the images on them were not representative of who my friend and I were as black women."

After looking closely at the greeting card industry, Mitchell-Raptakis felt that she had identified a niche — a narrow segment of the market that is overlooked by larger companies. The greeting card market is huge — Americans sent about 7 billion greeting cards in one recent year, spending about $7.5 billion, according to the Greeting Card Association. Mitchell-Raptakis decided to try to capture part of that market.

Following Her Heart

Mitchell-Raptakis soon decided to produce a line of greeting cards aimed at African-American women. "I wanted to manufacture my own cards for several reasons," she explains. "First, I was passionate about them! These were the cards that I would have wanted to receive. Second, I was always conscious of where I came from. I'm the granddaughter of sharecroppers and thought about the limited opportunities my ancestors had. I wanted to do this because they couldn't. Third, I wanted to reinvent myself and be challenged in my work. I needed to expand my horizons. Lastly, I wanted to break down the traditional definition of what an entrepreneur looked like and be a positive role model for the kids in my old neighborhood."

At first, Mitchell-Raptakis wanted to use quotations on the cards from famous African-American women, including Maya Angelou, Bessie and Sadie Delaney, Toni Morrison, and Oprah Winfrey. (For more information, see entries on Angelou in *Biography Today*, April 1993; the Delaney sisters in *Biography Today*, Sep. 1999; Morrison in *Biography Today*, Jan. 1994; and Winfrey in *Biography Today*, April 1992, and *Biography Today Business Leaders*, Vol. 1.) She wrote to the Delaney sisters' agent and asked for permission to use their words, but was turned down. She soon learned that any famous person would want royalties for the use of their thoughts. Mitchell-Raptakis didn't have the money to pay for royalties, so she scrapped her original plan. Instead, she decided to write her own messages on each card. She used forthright and natural phrases that were common and familiar in African-American culture. "These cards reflect the black experience and feature phrases that have been around in our community for generations," she stated. "The text is short and to the point, in the same way sisters usually speak with one another."

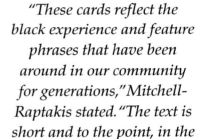

"These cards reflect the black experience and feature phrases that have been around in our community for generations,"Mitchell-Raptakis stated."The text is short and to the point, in the same way sisters usually speak with one another."

Then Mitchell-Raptakis teamed up with Fred Harper, a Brooklyn artist whose work had appeared in both New York and national publications, including *Sports Illustrated* and *Essence*. After consulting with Mitchell-Raptakis about her vision for the greeting card series, Harper created artwork featuring bold colors and striking depictions of African Americans. "I wanted a diversity of black women to be depicted in my cards — reflecting the diversity within our culture," she says. "Our hair texture and styles, varied skin tones, creative sense of fashion, and unique vernacular are represented in these cards. . . . I wanted us to see ourselves in all the facets." She took photographs of her friends and gave them to Harper, who incor-

A few words of wisdom:
1. A hard head gets a soft backside
2. God doesn't like ugly and He doesn't care for beauty
3. Every shut eye ain't sleep, every good bye ain't gone

Interior: No matter how old you get, don't forget what Mama taught you. Happy Birthday!

porated some of those images: a wedding scene of her good friends appears on a wedding congratulations card, and Mitchell-Raptakis's own image appears on a birthday card featuring a young girl with words of wisdom.

The next stage of the project was to find out if the cards would appeal to black consumers. As she developed the cards, Mitchell-Raptakis showed them to women she met in the hair salon, the grocery checkout line, on the subway, and various other places, in order to get objective opinions. She contacted African-American card and gift shops in Brooklyn and asked if they would be interested in purchasing the cards for their shops. Each card buyer gave her an order, which encouraged her even more. But there were so many obstacles. She didn't have the money to produce the cards, a commercial printer to manufacture the cards, or knowledge about starting a new business. Reluctantly, she put the project on hold for several years.

"I wanted a diversity of black women to be depicted in my cards — reflecting the diversity within our culture," Mitchell-Raptakis noted. *"Our hair texture and styles, varied skin tones, creative sense of fashion, and unique vernacular are represented in these cards. . . . I wanted us to see ourselves in all the facets."*

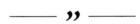

Creating the Dream

Then in January 1999 she watched an Oprah Winfrey show with Iyanla Vanzant, who talked about the struggles of her life. She then recited a poem by Patrick Overton that made Mitchell-Raptakis sit up in her chair. "When you walk to the edge of all the light you have and take that first step into the darkness of the unknown, you must believe one of two things will happen: There will be something solid for you to stand upon or you will be taught how to fly." The poem motivated her to take the next step and fortified her belief that God was instrumental in her plan. She felt so strongly about greeting cards for African-American women that she decided to put her faith and her plans into action.

Her family and friends supported her greeting card idea with spiritual, emotional, and physical support, while her mother provided much needed financial support. "It was so important to have such a wonderful support network," Mitchell-Raptakis reveals. "These were the people who believed in me when all I had was a dream. They believed in me when I have been low on faith."

In addition to such support, Mitchell-Raptakis needed the help of a team of experienced advisors. She found a greeting card consultant who taught her the basics about starting a greeting card business—including pricing, distribution, product design, major trade shows, and getting paid. She found a lawyer who specialized in intellectual property and applied for a trademark for the name "It's a Sista Thing!"™ She found an accountant and set up a corporation for The LDC Design Co., Inc. She found a printer who had experience in manufacturing greeting cards and the ability to store and ship her cards.

"It's a Sista Thing!"™

In 1999 Mitchell-Raptakis formally introduced her line of greeting cards—called "It's a Sista Thing!"™—at the National Stationery Show. The series of 24 cards spoke directly to African-American women, offering messages of encouragement, sympathy, and joy, along with birthday, wedding, and holiday greetings. Some examples from the line include:

- "Jumping the broom," a wedding card depicting a couple in traditional African dress preparing to step over a broom lying on the ground (part of the marriage ritual in some African cultures).

- "To the man I love," a Father's Day card illustrated with an image of a black man in dreadlocks with a baby sleeping on his chest.

- "A Christmas letter to Jesus," a holiday card picturing a boy writing at a table in front of a Christmas tree.

- "A few words of wisdom," a birthday card featuring the greeting, "No matter how old you get, don't forget what Mama taught you!"

"The first day I participated in the National Stationery Show was one of the most exciting days of my life," Mitchell-Raptakis observes. "I had attended the National Stationery Show as a visitor since 1983 and always felt that I didn't belong there. But my first day as a participant in the show gave me an extreme boost of confidence. This was my show. I was so happy to be there. The cards even created a 'buzz' among the other African-American card manufacturers and some of them came around to visit my booth and see my cards. The vice president of one large card manufacturer stopped by the booth, nodded, and said he liked the idea. I was ecstatic."

"It's a Sista Thing!"™ cards soon began to catch on in New York and New Jersey. Mitchell-Raptakis managed sales and distribution of the line herself, taking full responsibility for getting the cards into stores. She eventually succeeded in placing her products in more than 80 retail outlets, al-

———— **"** ————

*"My first day as a partici-
pant in the show gave me an
extreme boost of confidence.
This was my show. I was so
happy to be there. The cards
even created a 'buzz' among
the other African-American
card manufacturers and some
of them came around to visit
my booth and see my cards.
The vice president of one
large card manufacturer
stopped by the booth, nodded,
and said he liked the idea.
I was ecstatic."*

———— **"** ————

*Mitchell-Raptakis introduced her
greeting card line at the 1999 National
Stationery Show.*

though the majority of her customers were small specialty bookstores and stationery shops. She also made her cards available on the Internet.

Winning the Louie Award

Mitchell-Raptakis and her company received a big boost in 2001. She entered one of her cards in a contest sponsored by the Greeting Card Association. The top prize was the prestigious Louie Award. Named after German print-er Louis Prang, who is credited with introducing color lithography to the United States card industry, the award is considered the greeting card indus-try's equivalent to the film industry's Oscar.

For the contest, Mitchell-Raptakis entered an inspirational card that fea-tured an image of abolitionist Sojourner Truth on the cover and an original poem entitled "Your Spirit Will Not Be Broken" in the interior. The card celebrates the perseverance of past generations of African Americans who struggled against adversity to create a better future for their children.

More than 1,100 cards from 160 companies were entered in competition for the prize. Judges evaluated each card individually. "Your Spirit Will Not

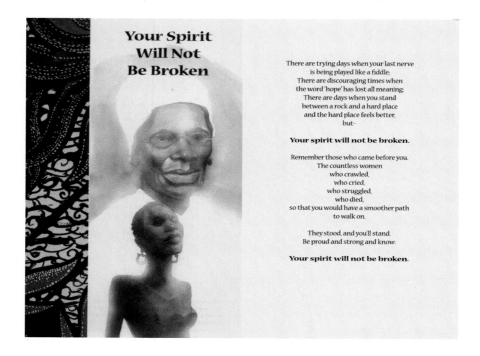

Your Spirit Will Not Be Broken

There are trying days when your last nerve
is being played like a fiddle;
There are discouraging times when
the word 'hope' has lost all meaning;
There are days when you stand
between a rock and a hard place
and the hard place feels better,
but–

Your spirit will not be broken.

Remember those who came before you.
The countless women
who crawled,
who cried,
who struggled,
who died,
so that you would have a smoother path
to walk on.

They stood, and you'll stand.
Be proud and strong and know:

Your spirit will not be broken.

Be Broken" was selected as the winner of the prestigious Louie Award in three categories: friendship, encouragement, and general. Judges cited its originality, impact, artistry, harmony, "sendability," and value. Mitchell-Raptakis attributed the success of the card to her creative process. "I send cards that I would like to get to encourage me," she reveals, "and 'Your Spirit Will Not Be Broken' is the card that I needed, so I had to create it."

Attending the Louie Award ceremony, Mitchell-Raptakis was honored to be part of a group of such talented people in an industry she loved so much. When her category was called and her card was announced as the winner, she was overwhelmed. It had been a long journey of faith and determination.

Growing Pains

Mitchell-Raptakis eventually hopes to expand the "It's a Sista Thing!"™ line beyond greeting cards into calendars, stationery, and other items. She feels just as strongly about the need for her products as she did in the beginning. "If you don't have that one girlfriend who you can tell things to or who you know can lift you up, you're in a bad state," she explains. "I do think of my friends when I create these cards: What will make somebody laugh? What will they want to hear in the way of encouragement? What kind of card can I send them just to say that I love them?"

Even though her cards have gained an enthusiastic following, Mitchell-Raptakis admits that she has experienced periods of doubt and discouragement. Since she spent so much money developing, printing, and marketing the cards, it took a long time for her business to make a profit. In fact, Mitchell-Raptakis continued working at her "day job" in book publishing through 2003. "I was going through some strategy sessions with other business owners, and everything with their businesses was great," she recalled. "They were making money, and here I was, still with my day job and not making money."

Mitchell-Raptakis is not sure what the future holds for her and her company. She faces difficult decisions about whether to expand her business beyond the level of a "one-woman shop." She has tried to prepare herself to do so by taking business courses in such subjects as marketing, licensing, branding, and financial strategy. But she admits that competing against greeting card giants like Hallmark and American Greetings is quite a challenge.

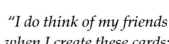

"I do think of my friends when I create these cards: What will make somebody laugh? What will they want to hear in the way of encouragement? What kind of card can I send them just to say that I love them?"

Despite the struggles, Mitchell-Raptakis says that being an entrepreneur has been very rewarding. "I have learned so much," she noted. "Creating these cards has been a labor of love and a journey of faith. It is my hope that 'It's a Sista Thing!'™ cards will connect African Americans to one another in a meaningful and positive way."

MARRIAGE AND FAMILY

Mitchell-Raptakis was married in 1981, but that marriage ended in divorce in 1993. She married Dimitrios Peter Raptakis, an accountant, on May 27, 2000. They live in East Stroudsbourg, Pennsylvania.

HOBBIES AND OTHER INTERESTS

Mitchell-Raptakis is a Christian and an active member in her church. She believes it is part of her mission to encourage others. In her free time, she enjoys a range of creative activities. She designs handmade cards, silk floral baskets, handmade books, and framed photo collages. She is writing a book of spiritual encouragement for women who have experienced domestic violence. She plans to write a children's book about her favorite cat, Buddy, who passed away. She also loves dancing and listening to music. Some of her favorite recording artists are Donnie McClurkin, Cece Winans, Brooklyn Tabernacle, Michael W. Smith, Babbie Mason, Avalon, Stevie Wonder, and others. She also enjoys going to movies with her husband.

HONORS AND AWARDS

Louis Award: 2001, in the friendship/encouragement/general category, for the Sojourner Truth Card

FURTHER READING

Periodicals

Essence, Mar. 2000, p.64
New York Amsterdam News, July 11, 2001, p.15
New York Daily News, Mar. 22, 2000, Suburban, p.6
USA Today, Mar. 19, 2003, p.B7

Online Articles

http://www.wibo.org
(*WIBO Word,* "Connect with Alumni Spotlight: Karen Mitchell-Raptakis of Karen & Co.," Spring 2003)

Other

Additional information for this biographical profile was gathered from material supplied by Karen Mitchell-Raptakis.

ADDRESS

Karen Mitchell-Raptakis
Karen and Company Greeting Cards
P.O. Box 972
East Stroudsburg, PA 18301

WORLD WIDE WEB SITE

http://www.sistathingcards.com

Queen Noor 1951-

American-Born Queen of Jordan
Author of the International Best-Seller *Leap of Faith:
Memoirs of an Unexpected Life*

BIRTH

Queen Noor al Hussein was born Lisa Najeeb Halaby on
August 23, 1951, in Washington, D.C. Her father, Najeeb Elias
Halaby, was a prominent Arab-American airline executive and
attorney who served as director of the Federal Aviation Administration under President John F. Kennedy. Her mother,
Doris (Carlquist) Halaby, was a homemaker. She has a younger brother, Christian, and a younger sister, Alexa.

In 1978 Lisa Halaby adopted the name Noor al Hussein, which means "Light of Hussein" in Arabic, when she married Hussein ibn Talal, king of the Middle Eastern nation of Jordan. She also became a Jordanian citizen at this time, relinquishing her American citizenship. In alphabetical listings, her name is commonly found under Noor al Hussein, Queen of Jordan.

YOUTH

The Halaby family moved around a lot during Lisa's youth to accommodate her father's frequent job changes. When Lisa was two years old, they moved from Washington, D.C., to New York City. By the time she was ready for kindergarten, they had relocated again, to southern California. "We moved often during my childhood, and the constant changes reinforced my natural reserve," she remembered in her book *Leap of Faith.* "Time and again, I would find myself on the outside looking in — watching, studying, learning — having to familiarize myself with unfamiliar people and communities." At one point, her mother became so concerned about Lisa's shyness around other children that she consulted a child psychologist.

> "We moved often during my childhood, and the constant changes reinforced my natural reserve," Queen Noor remembered in her book **Leap of Faith.** "Time and again, I would find myself on the outside looking in — watching, studying, learning — having to familiarize myself with unfamiliar people and communities."

The Halabys spent five years in California. Lisa particularly enjoyed living in Santa Monica, where the family home offered a spectacular view of the Pacific Ocean. She liked exploring the outdoors on her own. She also spent a great deal of time combing through the books in her father's extensive library, reading about exotic places around the world. "I would flip through copies of *National Geographic* and gaze longingly at the globe that helped me chart my parents' international trips," she recalled.

In 1961 the Halabys returned to Washington, D.C., so that Lisa's father could become director of the Federal Aviation Administration (FAA) under President Kennedy. Ten-year-old Lisa felt inspired by Kennedy, whom she met at his inauguration. She was especially attracted to the young president's emphasis on service to less privileged communities and countries.

Najeeb Halaby, father to the future Queen Noor, was appointed by
President John F. Kennedy to be director of the Federal Aviation Administration.
Halaby is shown here being sworn in as President Kennedy looks on.

For example, Kennedy established an international service organization called the Peace Corps in order to encourage Americans to spend time in developing nations helping to fight poverty, hunger, illiteracy, and other problems. Lisa was fascinated by the program and always wanted to become a Peace Corps volunteer. "I didn't dream of being a fairy-tale princess," she noted.

Sadly, President Kennedy was assassinated in 1963. Najeeb Halaby continued to head the FAA under the new president, Lyndon B. Johnson. Halaby resigned in 1965 to take a job in the private sector with Pan Am World Airways. The family then moved back to New York City.

EDUCATION

Lisa Halaby attended exclusive private schools for most of her education. During her father's tenure as director of the FAA, she attended the prestigious National Cathedral School for Girls in Washington, D.C. She struggled to fit in during her awkward teen years. "[I was] tall for my age, scrawny and awkward, and dependent on Coke-bottle-thick glasses," she recalled. When her father first went to work for Pan Am and the family moved to New York City, Lisa attended the Chapin School. She did not like the sheltered environment at the school, which felt "like a strait jacket" to the idealistic teenager. "The world was held at arm's length at Chapin, with no student involvement in the debate over Vietnam or the civil rights movement or, indeed, anything that smacked of dissent," she noted.

Halaby spent her last two years of high school at Concord Academy in Massachusetts, where she excelled in sports and worked on the school newspaper and yearbook. During the summers, she toured Europe with student groups. Looking back, she praised Concord Academy for challenging her to become a better student and person. "Academic life was extremely stimulating, and expectations were high, but more important to me, the school placed a high premium on individualism and personal responsibility," she remembered.

——— " ———

"I needed time and space to set my own priorities and to discover if I could survive on my own," Queen Noor explained. "That's one of my fondest memories, because it gave me an enormous amount of self-confidence to learn that I didn't need to depend on anyone — a husband, a father, my family — to support me. It taught me that I could take care of myself."

——— " ———

After graduating from high school in 1969, Halaby considered returning to California to attend Stanford University. But then she was accepted into the first co-ed class to enter Princeton University in New Jersey. She eagerly took advantage of the opportunity to become one of the first women to attend the prestigious Ivy League college. Shortly after her first semester got underway, her father was named president and chief executive officer of Pan Am. To her surprise, the media attention surrounding her father's promotion led some fellow students to harass her about her Arab background.

In 1971 Halaby took a year off from college to live on her own in Aspen, Colorado. She worked as a waitress and spent her spare time skiing and studying photography at the Institute of the Eye. "I needed time and space to set my own priorities and to discover if I could survive on my own," she explained. "That's one of my fondest memories, because it gave me an enormous amount of self-confidence to learn that I didn't need to depend on anyone — a husband, a father, my family — to support me. It taught me that I could take care of myself."

Halaby returned to Princeton the following year with renewed energy and focus. She became even more active in social causes and human rights issues, participating in fasts and other nonviolent protests against the Vietnam War. She also chose a new course of study — architecture and urban planning — that she felt would enable her to serve the needs of society. "I loved it," she remembered. "It was a captivating, multidisciplinary approach to understanding and addressing the most basic needs of individuals and communities." Halaby earned her bachelor's degree from Princeton in 1974.

CAREER HIGHLIGHTS

Experiencing the Middle East as a Young Architect

After graduating from college, Halaby took a job with Llewlyn-Davis, a British architecture firm specializing in urban development. Part of the job's appeal was that it offered opportunities to see the world. Her first assignment took her to Australia, and then she was sent to Iran to help modernize the capital city of Tehran. During her time in Iran, Halaby found herself captivated by the history and culture of the Middle East. She also became aware of what she described as "a fundamental lack of understanding in the West, especially in the United States, of Middle Eastern culture and the Muslim faith."

In 1976 the government of Jordan hired Halaby's father to help restructure its airline system. She went along and helped design a training facility at Arab Air University. From the time of her first visit to the capital city of Amman, she fell in love with Jordan. "On that first trip, I explored Amman on foot," she remembered in her book. "Shepherds crossed the downtown streets with their flocks, herding them from one grassy area to another. They were such an ordinary part of life in Amman that no one honked or lost their patience waiting for the streets to clear; animals and their minders had the right of way. I wandered through the marketplace admiring the beautiful inlaid mother-of-pearl objects — frames, chests, and backgammon boards — as well as the cobalt blue, green, and amber vases known as Hebron glass."

During her time in Jordan, Halaby was pleased to have an opportunity to meet the nation's ruler, King Hussein. They first met in January 1977 at a ceremony honoring Jordan's purchase of its first Boeing 747 jet plane. Halaby took a picture of the king greeting her father at this ceremony. Toward the end of that year, she returned to the United States. "I never imagined that I would be returning to Jordan just three months later," she said, "nor did I have any inkling of how fateful that return would be." (For more information on King Hussein, see *Biography Today*, April 1999.)

Map of the
Middle
East with
detail of
Jordan and
Israel.

Halaby had returned to the U.S. with the intention of studying journalism at Columbia University in New York City. But she unexpectedly received a job offer to serve as director of planning and design projects for Royal Jordanian Airlines. She jumped at the chance to return to Amman and to explore further her Arab heritage. "I can't explain why, but going there was something I knew I had to do," she stated. "I wanted to let it become a part of me, and I wanted to become part of it. It was the Arab blood in me that I identified with and that I wanted to discover."

Jordan and King Hussein

When Halaby returned to Jordan in early 1978, she committed herself to living and working in a small, developing nation that has a proud but often troubled history. Jordan, which is about the same size geographically as the state of Indiana, is located in the heart of the Middle East. It is surrounded by Syria, Iraq, Saudi Arabia, and Israel. Jordan's modern history begins in the early 20th century. Before World War I, much of the Middle East was part of the Ottoman Empire, which had been ruled by Turkish sultans for centuries. During World War I, the Ottoman Turks were allied with the Germans. When they were defeated and the Ottoman Empire crumbled, Great Britain was given the task of governing parts of the Middle East. The area eventually became 11 Arab nations, including Transjordan, founded in 1921. Its first king was Abdullah I, King Hussein's grandfather. In 1946 the country gained its independence from Great Britain and was renamed the Hashemite Kingdom of Jordan.

Two years later, in 1948, the United Nations created the nation of Israel as a homeland for all Jewish people. After World War II and the horrors of the Holocaust, when Nazis systematically murdered some six million Jews, Jewish people felt the need for a land of their own where they would be safe from persecution. The part of the Middle East that became Israel was also home to the Palestinians, an Arab people whose ancestors had lived in the region since ancient times. The creation of Israel angered many Arabs, in part because it displaced the Palestinian people, creating millions of refugees. Jordan and four of its neighbors went to war against Israel shortly after the Jewish nation was formed. The war lasted nine months before Israel defeated the Arab armies.

Even though the Arabs lost the war, Jordan captured part of Israel called the West Bank. This area along the Jordan River was home to 500,000 Palestinians, and it encompassed Jerusalem and Bethlehem—which contain holy sites for Christians, Jews, and Muslims. Once the war ended, thousands more Palestinians fled from Israel and became refugees in Jordan. King Abdullah struggled to maintain control of the country as Palestinians suddenly made up more than half of Jordan's population. Some of the displaced Palestinians formed a group called the Palestine Liberation Organization (PLO) with the purpose of reclaiming lost territory from Israel and establishing an independent Palestinian state. Until his death in 2004, Yasir Arafat was the leader of the PLO. (For more information on Arafat, see *Biography Today,* Sep. 1994, and Updates in the Annual Cumulations for 1994, 1995, 1996, 1997, 1998, 2000, 2001, and 2002; in addition, an obituary on Arafat will be featured in *Biography Today* in 2005.)

"I can't explain why, but going [to Jordan] was something I knew I had to do,"Queen Noor stated. "I wanted to let it become a part of me, and I wanted to become part of it. It was the Arab blood in me that I identified with and that I wanted to discover."

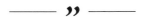

From the time of his birth in 1935, Hussein ibn Talal was prepared to become the leader of Jordan someday. After all, he was a 42nd-generation direct descendant of the Prophet Muhammad, founder of the Islamic religion. His family line, known as the Hashemites, had ruled Jordan since its founding. Hussein was educated at exclusive schools in Jordan, Egypt, and England. He also spent a great deal of time accompanying his grandfather and observing his official duties. In 1951 King Abdullah was assassinated by a Palestinian extremist while attending a ceremony in Jerusalem. Hussein, who was standing by his grandfather's side at the time, was hit as well. But the bullet harmlessly bounced off of a medal he was wearing on his chest.

Hussein's father, Talal, was named king of Jordan immediately following Abdullah's death. But Talal suffered from schizophrenia, and the pressures of the position soon made his mental illness worsen to the point that he could no longer rule. Hussein thus took over as king of Jordan in 1952, at the age of 16. He soon became known as a moderate ruler who placed a strong emphasis on education and development. But critics claimed that he was too easily influenced by the United States, which was unpopular in large parts of the Arab world due to its support for Israel. In 1967 Jordan joined Syria and Egypt in another war against Israel. This conflict became known as the Six-Day War because Israel prevailed so quickly. During the war, Israel regained control over the West Bank, which contained half of Jordan's population and much of its industrial capacity. Unhappy with Hussein's loss of the West Bank, Palestinian extremists tried to overthrow the king in a 1970 civil war.

———— " ————

"I was unsure I would be exactly what he needed, that I wouldn't be a hindrance, being relatively new to Jordan and because it did happen fairly quickly," Queen Noor acknowledged. *"I had lived an independent life, traveled in many different countries. I had a free, open spirit. Would I have the self-discipline necessary to make a good wife for a king?"*

———— " ————

Over the next few years, King Hussein managed to win the civil war and strengthen his rule. In 1974 he made an agreement with the PLO that helped ease tensions with Jordan's Palestinian population. Jordan gave up its claims on the West Bank, which remained under Israeli military control, and recognized the Palestinians as rightful owners of the disputed territory. Following this agreement, Jordan enjoyed a period of increased stability and economic growth. Over the succeeding years, King Hussein emerged as a leading figure in Middle Eastern affairs. He consistently sought ways to make peace with Israel while also securing greater rights for the Palestinians.

Becoming the Queen of Jordan

When Halaby returned to Jordan to become the director of planning and design projects for Royal Jordanian Airlines, the 42-year-old king was mourning the death of his third wife, Queen Alia, who had been killed in a helicopter crash in February 1977. In the spring of 1978, the 26-year-old American accompanied her father to a meeting at the royal palace. King Hussein enjoyed her company and invited her to lunch the next day.

Queen Noor and King Hussein on their wedding day, June 15, 1978, as they emerge from the wedding ceremony for the cutting of the cake.

Halaby spent that entire day with him and gave him advice on renovating the palace. Before long it became clear that the king's interest in Halaby extended beyond friendship. She was surprised but also flattered by the attention. "He was a *king*," she noted. "I was just, you know, a normal person."

King Hussein spent the next several weeks courting Halaby. They spoke on the phone for hours, and she visited the palace often. They both worked hard to keep their relationship a secret. In fact, the king sometimes came to meet her on a motorcycle so they could spend time alone together. After just two months of dating, King Hussein asked Lisa Halaby to marry him. She initially expressed doubts about her ability to become a queen. "I was unsure I would be exactly what he needed, that I wouldn't be a hindrance, being relatively new to Jordan and because it did happen fairly quickly," she acknowledged. "I had lived an independent life, traveled in many different countries. I had a free, open spirit. Would I have the self-discipline necessary to make a good wife for a king?"

Halaby recognized that she would face numerous challenges as King Hussein's wife. He was 16 years older, for example, and had already been married three times (his first two marriages ended in divorce). He had eight children—several of whom were almost Halaby's age, and three of whom were quite young and needed a mother. She also worried that the people of Jordan would have trouble accepting her because she had been born in the United States and did not speak much Arabic.

Yet Halaby ultimately allowed her emotions to overcome her caution. She had fallen in love with the charming king, so she agreed to be his wife. "When you're young and in love," she sighed. "I didn't stand aside, detach myself from the current of feeling, to consider the implications." They were married on June 15, 1978, at Zaharan Palace, the home of King Hussein's mother. The king gave his new bride the name Noor al Hussein because she brought light back into his life. Queen Noor became the first American-born queen of an Arab Muslim country. She also became the first woman in the history of the Hashemite family to attend her own wedding. (According to Jordanian tradition, marriage ceremonies are attended only by men, with a male relative representing the bride.)

> *"I admired Islam's emphasis on a believer's direct relationship with God, the fundamental equality of rights of all men and women, and the reverence for the Prophet Muhammad as well as all the Prophets and messengers who came before him, since Adam, to Abraham, Moses, Jesus, and many others. Islam calls for fairness, tolerance, and charity," Queen Noor explained. "I was attracted, too, by its simplicity and call for justice. Islam is a very personal belief system."*

Shortly before the wedding took place, Queen Noor converted to Islam. She had nominally been raised as a Christian, but she had never been baptized. Some people criticized her decision, claiming that she adopted the king's religion out of duty rather than true faith, but she said that she felt a real affinity for Islam. "I admired Islam's emphasis on a believer's direct relationship with God, the fundamental equality of rights of all men and women, and the reverence for the Prophet Muhammad as well as all the Prophets and messengers who came before him, since Adam, to Abraham, Moses, Jesus, and many others. Islam calls for fairness, tolerance, and charity," she explained. "I was attracted, too, by its simplicity and call for justice. Islam is a very personal belief system."

The wedding attracted a great deal of coverage in the international media. Many reporters seized upon the "fairy-tale" aspect of the union between a

The king and queen.

young American and a Middle Eastern king. But Queen Noor found that her new life did not really resemble a fairy tale. She worked hard to be a good stepmother to the king's eight children. She struggled to adjust to the loss of her privacy, as she suddenly found herself surrounded by body-guards at all times. Some citizens of Jordan viewed her with suspicion, questioning whether an American made a suitable wife for their king. Arabic television and newspapers followed her every move, ready to pounce on anything they viewed as a shortcoming. Some claimed that she was too ambitious, for example, while others criticized her for spending too much money. "All of a sudden, I was a wife, a queen, a mother," she re-membered. "All of a sudden I was inspected and analyzed."

Queen Noor tried to take the attention in stride. She pointed out that she needed time to determine the best ways of dealing with her unique posi-tion. "I'm pioneering a role here, as my husband's wife and queen in an ever-changing world, in a developing country that is in some ways back-ward, in a region that is extremely turbulent," she stated. "I am constantly questioning, as I know he is, the best way to approach certain tasks that we've set for ourselves, whether in social development or international relations or raising a family."

Emerging as a Humanitarian Activist

Once she settled into her new role, Queen Noor emerged as a leading activist in humanitarian causes. She started out working within Jordan to improve the people's health, education, and welfare. For example, the former architect helped convince Jordan to adopt a national professional building code. She also led efforts to preserve Jordan's architectural history through the National Committee for Public Buildings and Architectural Heritage. Queen Noor personally visited Palestinian refugee camps to ensure that they were safe and sanitary, and she also participated in child immunization campaigns throughout the country. In the early years of her reign, she often drove herself to remote villages in a jeep, listening to music by Fleetwood Mac or Bruce Springsteen along the way.

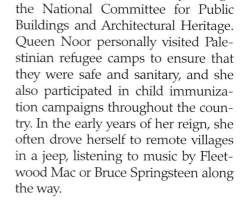

"If you provide opportunities for women, you transform the future prospect of the family and the community," Queen Noor explained. "An educated woman is going to impart her knowledge. Her children are going to be better educated, better able to play a role in their communities, [and] less likely to fall into the trap of the kind of hopelessness and despair that leads to extremism."

Queen Noor directed some of her efforts toward improving relations between Arab countries and the Western world. "I'm going to continue to the best of my abilities to develop my own understanding and experience, to be a better spokesman for the Arab world, and for Jordan in particular," she stated. "I pray I can be one small block to build greater understanding for everyone in the area."

Queen Noor also worked tirelessly to promote women's rights. "If you provide opportunities for women, you transform the future prospect of the family and the community," she explained. "An educated woman is going to impart her knowledge. Her children are going to be better educated, better able to play a role in their communities, [and] less likely to fall into the trap of the kind of hopelessness and despair that leads to extremism." She often appeared in public wearing beautiful handmade clothing in order to demonstrate her support for traditional Jordanian women's crafts.

Queen Noor, shown here visiting an orphanage, won the respect of many Jordanians for her commitment to charitable causes.

Over the years, Queen Noor won over the people of Jordan with her commitment to charitable work in the areas of child welfare, environmental protection, and culture and the arts. She started children's reading programs, created parks to promote recreation and tourism, and established the first children's museum in the Arab world. She also initiated the National Handicrafts Development Foundation and the Jerash Festival for Culture and Arts. Queen Noor became actively involved in numerous international organizations over the years, including the World Conservation Union, World Wildlife Fund, International Commission on Missing Persons, Women Waging Peace, Future Harvest, and the International Campaign to Ban Landmines. She earned numerous awards and honorary degrees for her charity work.

Speaking Out on Political Issues

In 1980 Queen Noor returned to the United States for the first time since her marriage. She and her husband met with President Jimmy Carter and his wife, Rosalynn Carter. Later that year Queen Noor gave birth to her first child, a son named Hamzah. She and the king had three more children together over the next few years: another son, Hashim, and two daughters,

119

Iman and Raiyah. As her own family grew, Queen Noor experienced some difficulty in dealing with the king's older children. In fact, in the mid-1980s they presented their father with a list of 54 grievances about her handling of family issues.

In 1990 the Middle East erupted in yet another military conflict when Iraq invaded Kuwait. Iraqi leader Saddam Hussein (no relation to King Hussein) invaded his tiny neighbor after the two countries failed to settle longstanding disputes over national boundaries, oil reserves, and other issues. Countries around the world condemned the invasion and called for Iraq to withdraw its troops from Kuwait. Many countries sent military forces to the region as part of a U.S.-led coalition against Iraq. This coalition included a number of Arab countries. (For more information on Saddam Hussein, see *Biography Today*, July 1992, and Updates in the Annual Cumulations for 1996, 2001, and 2002.)

> ————— **"** —————
>
> *King Hussein extolled his wife's virtues in a letter to the people of Jordan. "She brought happiness and cared for me during my illness with the utmost loving affection. She, the Jordanian, who belongs to this country with every fiber of her being, holds her head high in the defense and service of the country's interest. She, like me, also endured many anxieties and shocks, but always placed her faith in God and hid her tears behind smiles."*
>
> ————— **"** —————

King Hussein found himself in a difficult position following Iraq's invasion of Kuwait. He considered Saddam Hussein to be a personal friend, and he appreciated the Iraqi leader's strong defense of Palestinian interests. But he also respected Kuwait's status as an independent nation and expressed concern about Iraq's military aggression toward an Arab neighbor. The king tried desperately to remain neutral in the conflict. He traveled widely throughout the Middle East in an effort to negotiate a peaceful resolution to the crisis. He also met with Saddam Hussein and tried to convince him to withdraw his troops from Kuwait.

As it became clear that the U.S.-led coalition would go to war to force Iraq to withdraw from Kuwait, King Hussein refused to participate. He knew that Jordan's large Palestinian population approved of Saddam Hussein's actions, and he did not want to risk an uprising that would put his rule at risk. But the king's position proved to be very unpopular with the United

States as well as with the Arab members of the coalition. Many of these countries cut off trade with Jordan and refused to help King Hussein deal with the three million refugees who made their way into Jordan from Iraq and Kuwait before and during the 1991 Persian Gulf War.

Throughout this difficult political situation, Queen Noor often spoke out in defense of Jordan's position. She felt that her husband had been treated unfairly, when his only aim was to avoid a costly war. In September 1990 she met with Barbara Bush, the wife of U.S. President George Bush. The queen told the first lady that Jordan had always opposed Iraq's invasion of Kuwait and that King Hussein's position had been misrepresented. "I tried to explain the mounting concern in the Arab world about Iraqi civilian losses and desperate conditions. Mrs. Bush was unmoved. She was a political wife, and she was going to believe what she needed to believe," Queen Noor wrote in her memoirs. "I would continue to speak out after the war started about the humanitarian consequences of the war and the suffering of the people of Iraq, which evidently so angered Mrs. Bush that she sent a message to me through an American official that she considered me a traitor."

In January 1991 the coalition forces launched a major bombing campaign against Iraqi forces. This campaign, which lasted for nearly six weeks, took a devastating toll on both Iraq and Kuwait. The coalition then followed up with a ground assault that quickly succeeded in pushing Iraqi forces out of Kuwait.

Standing by the King

In 1992 doctors discovered a tumor in King Hussein's kidney that contained cancerous cells. Queen Noor traveled with her husband to the prestigious Mayo Clinic in Minnesota, where doctors removed the tumor along with one of the king's kidneys. The cancer scare made King Hussein more energized than ever to seek peace in the Middle East. Over the next few years he repaired Jordan's relationships with its neighbors as well as with the United States, and he gradually emerged as one of the leading statesmen in the Arab world. In 1993 the king played a key role in negotiations that resulted in an agreement between Israel and the PLO that provided for Palestinian self-rule in the West Bank and other Israeli-occupied territories. The following year Jordan entered into a peace agreement with Israel, ending a 46-year state of war between the neighboring countries.

In 1997 King Hussein developed non-Hodgkins lymphoma, a type of cancer that affects the lymphatic system, which circulates antibodies throughout the body to help it fight infection and disease. The following year

Queen Noor accompanied her husband to the Mayo Clinic for intensive treatment, including chemotherapy and a bone marrow transplant. In her book, she describes her initial despair at the prospect of losing her beloved husband. "I felt such fear, such bottomless anxiety at the thought of losing my husband, my best friend, my dearest love and inspiration that it threatened to paralyze me. For 20 years we had been husband and wife, father and mother, life partners through international crises and domestic turmoil in Jordan," she noted. "To lose this man would be a catastrophe on every level imaginable."

——— " ———

"The spiritual journey that began when I married my husband came to a head during his illness and with his loss,"Queen Noor wrote. "Islam was never a greater comfort to me than during that time. I was able to accept God's will and be at peace during and after the king's death in a way that I would never have been able to imagine."

——— " ———

Queen Noor spent six months in Minnesota with King Hussein while he underwent treatment. Despite his illness, he still managed to assist President Bill Clinton in arranging further peace negotiations between Israel and the Palestinians. By the end of 1998 it appeared that the king was free of cancer. Queen Noor took her husband back to Jordan in January 1999, where they were greeted by huge, enthusiastic crowds. During the next few weeks, King Hussein met with his younger brother, Crown Prince Hassan, to discuss the issue of succession. He decided that his eldest son, Abdullah, would replace his brother as successor to the throne. Some Jordanians criticized the king's decision and claimed that Queen Noor was behind the move, because it made it more likely that her own sons would eventually become king. But King Hussein noted that he and his brother had drifted apart in terms of their political philosophy, so he felt that his son would make a better ruler.

Just a few weeks after his triumphant return to Jordan, King Hussein's cancer returned. He and Queen Noor went back to the Mayo Clinic, where he underwent another bone marrow transplant. The operation was unsuccessful, however, and the queen made the difficult decision to bring her husband home to die. During his final days, Queen Noor and her daughters left the hospital in the middle of a rainstorm to meet with the crowd holding a vigil outside.

Jordan's King Abdullah II, second from left, Queen Rania, left, and Queen Noor, right, hold special Muslim prayers at King Hussein's grave in the royal cemetary in Amman.

King Hussein died on February 7, 1999, at the age of 63. Queen Noor stood by her husband throughout the ordeal of his cancer. When he died, her dignity and composure provided comfort to a grieving nation and earned her the respect of many Jordanian citizens. She noted in her book that her adopted religion helped her cope with her loss. "The spiritual journey that began when I married my husband came to a head during his illness and with his loss," she wrote. "Islam was never a greater comfort to me than during that time. I was able to accept God's will and be at peace during and after the king's death in a way that I would never have been able to imagine."

Shortly before he died, King Hussein extolled his wife's virtues in a letter to the people of Jordan. "She brought happiness and cared for me during my illness with the utmost loving affection. She, the Jordanian, who belongs to this country with every fiber of her being, holds her head high in the defense and service of the country's interest," he stated. "She, like me, also endured many anxieties and shocks, but always placed her faith in God and hid her tears behind smiles."

**Moving Forward and
Revisiting the Past**

Queen Noor's stepson Abdullah became king of Jordan upon her husband's death. For the next few years, Queen Noor stepped out of the public eye. She spent her time doing charity work and supporting her children as they pursued their education abroad.

In 2003 Queen Noor returned to the public spotlight with the publication of her book, *Leap of Faith: Memoirs of an Unexpected Life,* which became an international best-seller. The book recounts the story of her courtship and marriage, discusses the challenges she faced in adjusting to a different culture, and documents her husband's efforts to bring peace to the Middle East. It received a great deal of praise for providing an intimate, inside look at some of the important political events of the previous 25 years. But it was also criticized in some quarters for shortchanging the Jewish perspective on recent Middle East history.

Queen Noor explained that she wrote the book in order "to share my perspective on living in two different cultures. Like my husband, I have a conviction that there is much more that binds culture than separates us. I feel a responsibility to highlight our common ground so that both cultures can work together to resolve conflicts peacefully. My husband is the hero of the book; his search for peace is the central theme, and yet it's not meant to be a definitive historical or political account."

"Queen Noor offers a vastly informative and even fascinating memoir," wrote Brad Hooper in *Booklist.* "As the woman who stood behind one of the major players in the Middle East in the second half of the 20th century, Queen Noor brings a unique perspective to the contemporary history of the region." That view was echoed by Julie Salamon in the *New York Times Book Review.* "*Leap of Faith* fulfills its mandate of assuring ordinary readers that real-life fairy tales are suffused with pain as well as magic," said Salamon. "What emerges is a careful yet often revealing account of domestic adjustment and Middle East politics, as well as an affecting wifely portrait of King Hussein." Queen Noor donated all profits from the book to the

King Hussein Foundation, an organization that supports educational programs to promote peace and democracy in the Middle East.

Thanks in part to the success of her book, Queen Noor has emerged as an unofficial spokesperson for Arab political views in the United States. She spoke out in hopes of creating greater understanding between her two cultures, but in some cases her comments generated controversy. In interviews promoting her memoirs, for example, she offered her views on the 2003 U.S.-led invasion of Iraq, which succeeded in removing Saddam Hussein from power. "The United States has won military victories in Afghanistan and Iraq," she noted. "Now the question is, can America win the peace? It takes seconds to destroy something that might have taken centuries to build, and by this I mean not just buildings and monuments, but optimism, trust, and hope. The ability to compromise rests on these things. We've seen a mistaken notion among hardliners in Israel and Palestine — and sometimes in the United States, too — that security comes from guns and building walls. We are hopeful that the United States will apply its

"Leap of Faith *fulfills its mandate of assuring ordinary readers that real-life fairy tales are suffused with pain as well as magic,"wrote Julie Salamon in the* **NewYork Times Book Review.**

historic commitment to justice to this entire region. America can promote peace in the Middle East only if these principles are paramount. This is especially true in relation to the Arab-Israeli conflict, where America's credibility rests not just on its strength, but also on its wisdom and humanitarian ideals."

MARRIAGE AND FAMILY

Lisa Halaby married Hussein ibn Talal, king of Jordan, on June 15, 1978. They had four children together: His Royal Highness Prince Hamzah (born in 1980); His Royal Highness Prince Hashim (1981); Her Royal Highness Princess Iman (1983); and Her Royal Highness Princess Raiyah (1986). They also raised eight children from the king's three previous marriages: Princes Abdullah, Feisal, and Ali; and Princesses Alia, Zein, Aisha, Haya, and Abir Muheisen.

Queen Noor and King Hussein lived in Jordan's royal palace, but they also maintained homes in the United States and England. Following her hus-

Queen Noor shown with her husband and their four children in about 1986-87.

band's death in 1999, the queen began spending the majority of her time in Potomac, Maryland, to be near her daughters, who were attending school in the United States. She returned to Jordan for about one week out of every month to oversee her charitable foundations.

Five years after King Hussein's death, the media speculated about a romantic link between Queen Noor and Jim Kimsey, a multi-millionaire co-founder of America Online and prominent Washington-based philanthropist. But she claims that she has no plans to remarry. "Who am I going to marry?" she noted. "I've been married to a charming, attractive king."

HOBBIES AND OTHER INTERESTS

In her spare time, Queen Noor enjoys skiing, water skiing, sailing, horseback riding, reading, gardening, and photography.

SELECTED WRITINGS

Leap of Faith: Memoirs of an Unexpected Life, 2003

HONORS AND AWARDS

Grand Cordon of the Jeweled Al Nahda (Jordan): 1978
Grand Collar of Al Hussein bin Ali (Jordan): 1980
Global 500 Award (United Nations): 1995

FURTHER READING

Books

Collopy, Michael, and Jason Gardner, eds. *Architects of Peace: Visions of Hope in Words and Images,* 2000
Darraj, Susan Muaddi. *Queen Noor,* 2004 (juvenile)
Queen Noor. *Leap of Faith: Memoirs of an Unexpected Life,* 2003

Periodicals

Biography, Sep. 2003, p.44
Current Biography Yearbook, 1991
Good Housekeeping, Apr. 2003, p.125
Ms., Fall 2003, p.39
People, Mar. 1, 1999, p.54; June 9, 2003, p.115
Time, Mar. 29, 1999, p.50
Washington Post, Nov. 6, 1981, p.C1; June 19, 1999, p.C1; Mar. 2, 2004, p.C1
Washingtonian, Oct. 1999, p.50

Online Databases

Biography Resource Center Online, 2004, article from *Contemporary Authors Online,* 2003

ADDRESS

Office of Her Majesty Queen Noor
Bab Al Salam Palace
Amman, Jordan

E-mail: noor@queennoor.jo

WORLD WIDE WEB SITE

http://www.noor.gov.jo

Antonin Scalia 1936-
American Justice on the U.S. Supreme Court
Youngest Supreme Court Justice in U.S. History

BIRTH

Antonin Scalia (pronounced skah-LEE-a) was born on March 11, 1936, in Trenton, New Jersey. He was the only child of S. Eugene Scalia, a language professor of Sicilian heritage, and Catherine Panaro Scalia, a first-generation Italian-American who worked as a schoolteacher. Since early childhood, Antonin has been called "Nino" by many of his family and friends.

YOUTH

Scalia spent his early years in Trenton. When he was five his father secured a position as a professor of romance languages at Brooklyn College in New York City. The family subsequently moved to Queens, New York, a short commuting distance from the Brooklyn College campus. They lived there, nestled among a wide circle of relatives, through Scalia's teen years.

Both of Scalia's parents were proud members of the Catholic Church, and they raised their son to appreciate the importance of family and the value of religious faith. In addition, they created a home environment that encouraged learning and intellectual stimulation. Smart and curious from an early age, Scalia thrived under these conditions. "He would ask me such questions!" recalled one of his aunts. "He'd ask about the universe, about everything happening around. He floored me many times."

Scalia's youthful energy and intelligence impressed his father as well. "He was good at anything he did," recalled S. Eugene Scalia. "He played the piano when he was very young and I wondered how he managed to do so well and practice so little. He picked up the guitar in nothing at all. The minute I put him on a bicycle he took off, 'whoosh.'"

"He was good at anything he did," recalled Scalia's father. "He played the piano when he was very young and I wondered how he managed to do so well and practice so little. He picked up the guitar in nothing at all. The minute I put him on a bicycle he took off, 'whoosh.'"

EDUCATION

Scalia attended public school in New York City. For high school his parents enrolled him at Saint Francis Xavier, a Jesuit school in Manhattan. Scalia was a natural leader, both in the classroom and out. First in his class when he graduated in 1953, he also directed the school's marching band and played the title role in a school production of *MacBeth*. "He was brilliant, way above everybody else," recalled one high school classmate.

After earning his high school diploma, Scalia moved on to Georgetown University in Washington, D.C., where he studied history. He dazzled faculty and classmates alike with his affable manner, sharp wit, and intelligence. "[He was] not just bright," recalled former New Jersey Attorney General James Zazzali, who attended Georgetown at the same time. "He

A rather surpring shot of the future Supreme Court justice as MacBeth in a high school production, in a photo from the Xavier yearbook, about 1952-53.

was unbelievably brilliant." When he graduated from Georgetown in 1957 with a bachelor's degree in history, Scalia was class valedictorian — the graduating senior with the highest grade point average.

Scalia then enrolled at Harvard Law School, where he became editor of the prestigious *Harvard Law Review*. He became known around campus for his deeply conservative political beliefs. Scalia also became known for delivering spirited defenses of his beliefs in friendly debates with faculty and friends. "Conservative" political beliefs have traditionally emphasized low taxes, limited government services, and opposition to social change. After graduating with top honors in 1960 with his law degree, he explored Europe for several months. It was during these travels that he met and became engaged to Maureen McCarthy, his future wife.

CAREER HIGHLIGHTS

In 1961 Scalia accepted a job in Cleveland, Ohio, with Jones, Day, Cockley, and Reavis, the city's most prestigious law firm. He worked as an attorney in Cleveland until 1967, when he accepted a teaching position in the University of Virginia law program. In 1971 Scalia took his first formal step into the world of public service, accepting the position of general counsel to the White House Office of Telecommunications Policy in the administration of President Richard M. Nixon. In this position Scalia helped media industry leaders reach major agreements on cable television regulations and development.

In 1972 Scalia was appointed chairman of the Administrative Conference of the United States, a federal study group that examines legal and management issues affecting the executive branch of government. Over the ensuing months, a national scandal known as Watergate engulfed the Nixon administration. This scandal concerned revelations that members of Nixon's administration and re-election organization had planned a burglary at the headquarters of the Democratic National Committee in the Watergate office complex in Washington, D.C. These events occurred during the presidential campaign in 1972, when President Nixon was running for reelection. The burglary had been committed by staffers connected to the president's campaign, and it had occurred at the office of the Democratic Party. Even worse, high-ranking staffers had then tried to create a massive cover up to hide these illegal acts. Investigation of this burglary — by the press and by other government agencies — gradually centered on audiotapes and documents held by President Nixon himself.

By 1974 Watergate investigators and Nixon were locked in a bitter struggle for possession of these potentially incriminating tapes and documents. At the height of this battle, Scalia was named assistant attorney general in the Office of Legal Counsel at the U.S. Department of Justice. As such, he was part of the executive branch, like the president. In this position, his responsibilities included providing legal advice to the president on various issues affecting the Oval Office.

Shortly after joining the Department of Justice, Scalia told Nixon that the president — not the federal government — was the rightful owner of the Watergate tapes and documents. Scalia believed that the executive branch of the U.S. government should have the right to keep such information to itself. Nixon embraced this opinion and continued to withhold the tapes. Eventually, however, the U.S. Supreme Court (the judicial branch) rejected Nixon's position and demanded that he turn the tapes and documents over to investigators. Aware that the tapes contained proof that he had engaged in criminal activity and lied to the American people, Nixon resigned from office a few days later. He was the first president ever to resign from office.

A Growing Reputation in Conservative Circles

In January 1977 Scalia left the Justice Department to join the law faculty at the University of Chicago. Around this same time he was named a resident scholar at the American Enterprise Institute (AEI), a nationally known conservative "think tank" based in Washington, D.C. His affiliation with AEI reflected Scalia's growing reputation as one of the most brilliant and promising champions of conservativism in America.

Scalia enjoyed the next several years in Chicago. His family had grown so large by this time that he and his wife converted a former fraternity house into a home to raise their nine children. In the meantime, Scalia balanced his teaching duties with work as coeditor of two scholarly journals that promoted conservative economic and social policies.

There are a variety of philosophies that determine how legal experts interpret and create laws. Some judges follow the philosophy of "judicial activism," which gives judges a lot of freedom in deciding legal issues and interpreting the Constitution. But Scalia took a different approach, developing a reputation during this time as a disciple of the philosophy of "judicial restraint." This philosophy insists that judges should interpret legal questions according to very narrow readings of the Constitution, the Bill of Rights, and other laws. The philosophy of judicial restraint also holds that judges should never make legal decisions for the purpose of changing social and economic policies. In the view of Scalia and other believers in judicial restraint, policymaking in the social and economic arenas should be left entirely to Congressional lawmakers, as stated in the Constitution. Scalia championed this philosophy both in the classroom and in print. As he wrote several years later in his book *A Matter of Interpretation,* "Congress can enact foolish statutes as well as wise ones, and it is not for the courts to decide which is which and rewrite the former."

> "
>
> *"[Scalia believes that] laws mean what they actually say, not what legislators intended them to say but did not write into the law's text."*
> —*Amy Gutmann, preface to Antonin Scalia's book*
> A Matter of Interpretation
>
> "

A Rising Star in the Judicial Branch

In 1982 Scalia was appointed to the U.S. Court of Appeals for the Washington, D.C., circuit. This court is widely regarded as second in importance only to the U.S. Supreme Court. Because it's based in Washington, this court hears many cases in which the U.S. Congress, the executive branch, and various federal agencies are deeply involved.

Scalia's seat on the U.S. Court of Appeals gave him numerous opportunities to stake out his positions on various legal and social issues. As the months passed, it became clear that his conservative perspective on issues brought before the court was a pretty close match to that of the administration of President Ronald Reagan. For example, both Scalia and Reagan felt that the U.S. Constitution did not give Americans the right to abortion. They also shared a strong dislike for race-based affirmative action programs and championed private property rights.

By the mid-1980s, the Reagan administration's appreciation for Scalia and his conservative rulings was well-known. In fact, many observers predicted

In June 1986, President Ronald Reagan announced the retirement of Chief Justice Warren Burger (far right) and the nominations of Associate Justice William Rehnquist (second from right) to be chief justice and Scalia (far left) to be an associate justice.

that if President Reagan had an opportunity to fill a vacancy on the U.S. Supreme Court, Scalia would be one of the most likely candidates. As it turned out, this speculation proved to be right on target.

Joining the U.S. Supreme Court

In 1986 legendary Chief Justice Warren E. Burger retired from the U.S. Supreme Court. He was replaced as head of the court by longtime associate justice William Rehnquist. On June 24, 1986, meanwhile, the Reagan administration nominated Scalia to fill the vacancy.

Scalia was tremendously excited about the prospect of becoming a member of the highest court in the United States. But he knew that his nomination would first have to be confirmed by the U.S. Senate, in accordance with the rules of the Constitution. In September 1986 Scalia appeared before the Senate Judiciary Committee, which had the responsibility of making a recommendation for or against his confirmation to the larger Senate.

Prior to Scalia's appearance, many observers wondered if his conservative reputation would trigger attacks from liberal or moderate members of the committee. But Scalia's undeniable accomplishments and his thoughtful, good-humored personality won over the entire committee. His nomination was passed along to the Senate, and on September 17 he was confirmed by a 98-0 vote. Scalia thus became the first Italian-American ever to take a seat on the U.S. Supreme Court. At 50 years of age, he also became the youngest Supreme Court justice in U.S. history.

A seat on the nine-member Supreme Court is both a tremendous honor and a great responsibility. The court decides whether the laws made by all levels of government—federal, state, and local—follow the Constitution. The court accomplishes this by interpreting the provisions of the Constitution and applying its rules to specific legal cases. Because the Constitution lays out general rules, the court tries to determine their meaning and figure out how to apply them to modern situations. After the Justices select a case for review—and they accept fewer than about 100 of the 6,000 cases presented to them each year—they first will hear arguments by the two opposing sides. They begin discussing the case and take a preliminary vote to see which side has a majority of votes. Then one justice from the majority is assigned to write up the court's opinion. Drafting an opinion is complex and time-consuming, and the whole process can take over a year. The court's final opinion has tremendous importance, setting out a precedent that all lower courts and all levels of government throughout the United States are required to follow. The reasoning given in the opinion is also important, because it helps people understand the basis for the decision and how the ruling might apply to other cases in the future.

> "He gives clerks major research assignments and allows broad latitude in the first drafts of opinions," reported the **Washingtonian.** "The conservative Scalia frequently hires at least one liberal-to-moderate clerk to play devil's advocate."

Making His Mark

Scalia made an immediate splash upon joining the court. Legal analysts soon were praising his scholarship, his writing abilities (displayed in opinions on various cases brought before the court), and his engaging personality. One writer even stated that among the other judges, who can seem like silent gray pigeons on a railing, Scalia stood out like a colorful talking parrot.

Before long, promising young lawyers were fighting for the chance to serve as one of Scalia's clerks — the lawyers who work with the justices, doing research on upcoming cases and writing legal opinions. This keen competition for these seats derived from his reputation for constantly challenging his clerks to hone their legal skills and their minds. "He gives clerks major research assignments and allows broad latitude in the first drafts of opinions," reported the *Washingtonian.* "The conservative Scalia frequently hires at least one liberal-to-moderate clerk to play devil's advocate."

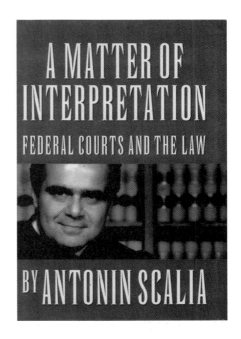

Scalia also made his guiding legal philosophy clearly known, both to his colleagues on the court and to the world at large. His philosophy, called textualism or originalism, is founded on the belief that the *original* meaning of the Constitution and other laws should continue to govern all legal judgments. Or, as Amy Gutmann summarized in the preface to Antonin Scalia's book *A Matter of Interpretation,* Scalia believes that "laws mean what they actually say, not what legislators intended them to say but did not write into the law's text."

Not surprisingly, this philosophy led Scalia to criticize judges who allow their modern-day "intellectual, moral, and personal perceptions" to override the "text and tradition" of the Constitution and other established laws. In his view, judges should always give greatest weight to the Constitution's original meaning, even if it seems unfair or wrong to modern Americans. Correcting these flaws is, according to Scalia, the responsibility of lawmakers in the executive and legislative branch of American government, not judges in the judiciary branch.

By the early 1990s, Scalia was viewed by many conservative political leaders, writers, and ordinary Americans as their "favorite" justice. After all, his opinions typically reflected their beliefs on such issues as church-state separation, abortion, affirmative action, privacy rights, and property rights. But he did not always side with conservatives. For example, his strong defense of the First Amendment, which ensures free speech for Americans, frustrated some conservative groups. Scalia cited the First Amendment when he voted with the majority in striking down a Texas law that prohibited the burning of the American flag.

In 1997 Scalia published an essay about his political beliefs called *A Matter of Interpretation: Federal Courts and the Law*. This essay, which was published side-by-side with commentaries from several legal scholars, was widely praised as an eloquent defense of the principle of "textualism." "[Scalia] projects a sanguine humor through a robust prose enlivened by sly sallies against what he sees as the gaps in the logic of the opposing camp. He is anything but the angry justice of popular myth," commented the *Wall Street Journal*. The *ABA Journal* offered similar praise, exclaiming that "as a writer of essays he is formidably persuasive, by turns seductive, fierce, funny, charming—and always brilliant."

> "To be able to write an opinion for oneself, without the need to accommodate, to any degree whatever, the more-or-less-differing views of one's colleagues; to address precisely the points of law that one considers important and no others; to express precisely the degree of quibble or foreboding or disbelief or indignation that one believes the majority's position should engender— that is indeed an unparalleled pleasure."

Scalia and His Colleagues

By the late 1990s, however, personal issues seemed to be playing a role on the court. Rumblings that Scalia was disliked by some of his colleagues threatened to overshadow his judicial philosophy and his widely admired skills as a writer and interrogator of attorneys presenting arguments before the court. His reputation as a friendly and engaging person at home and at play remained intact. But many court observers believed that Scalia had developed a bad habit of publicly ridiculing the legal opinions of other justices with whom he disagreed. "No other current justice shows as much contempt for colleagues," declared the *Dallas Morning News* in 1996. "When Mr. Scalia was named to the court 10 years ago, commentators predicted that his intellect and charm would help forge a conservative consensus. Instead, his embittered rhetoric and sarcastic humor drove away the others, except for Justice Clarence Thomas. Demonstrating no interest in consensus building, he revels in dissent. . . .

He places self-importance above the court's prestige as a governing institution — an institution that should be above petty, personal bickering."

Even conservative legal analysts voiced concern about Scalia's public attacks on some of the other justices. They typically agreed with his views, but worried that his blunt criticisms undermined his ability to convince a majority of justices to support rulings he favors. Scalia remained unapologetic about his outspoken ways, however. He also strongly defended his preference for writing his own legal opinions, rather than signing off on those penned by other justices: "To be able to write an opinion for oneself, without the need to accommodate, to any degree whatever, the more-or-less-differing views of one's colleagues; to address precisely the points of law that one considers important and no others; to express precisely the degree of quibble or foreboding or disbelief or indignation that one believes the majority's position should engender — that is indeed an unparalleled pleasure."

Growing Controversy

In the first years of the 21st century, Scalia's reputation as a brilliant conservative mind continued to flourish. But critics sharpened their attacks on him, accusing him of excessive pride and hypocrisy in some of his votes. For example, Scalia was part of the 5-4 court majority that called a halt to the disputed recount of voting in Florida during the 2000 presidential election. This ruling effectively gave the presidency to conservative Republican George W. Bush over Democratic candidate Al Gore. Critics charged that Scalia's vote in the court case *Bush v. Gore* was inconsistent with his previous conservative legal opinions on equal protection issues. "His opponents claim Scalia acted as a ruthless, self-serving politician who put his own boy in power when it looked like the other side might win," summarized *Commonweal.* Scalia and his supporters, though, contended that his vote was based on sound legal principles, not political considerations.

In subsequent months, Scalia's strongly worded opinions on a variety of issues attracted further controversy. He argued, for example, that all-male military schools should not have to open their doors to women, and he insisted that governmental institutions had the legal right to discriminate against gay people if they wished. These opinions were warmly praised by some Americans and harshly condemned by others.

In 2003 Scalia's sense of propriety and impartiality was repeatedly called into question by court watchers. One time, he gave a keynote dinner speech to a group waging a legal battle against gay rights — at the same time that

The Supreme Court in 2003. Front row, left to right: Antonin Scalia, John Paul Steven, Chief Justice William H. Rehnquist, Sandra Day O'Connor, and Anthony M. Kennedy. Back row, left to right: Ruth Bader Ginsburg, David Souter, Clarence Thomas, and Stephen Breyer.

he and other members of the Supreme Court were weighing an important gay rights case. Many considered this a conflict of interest.

On another occasion, Scalia went on a duck hunting vacation with Vice President Dick Cheney. The timing of this trip raised eyebrows even among some Scalia supporters, for it took place shortly before the Supreme Court was supposed to make an important ruling on a fierce legal battle between Cheney and various environmental and governmental watchdog groups. Afterward, Scalia strongly defended himself, stating that socializing should not be automatic grounds for disqualifying a judge from a pending case. But critics such as the *Nation* claimed that Scalia's decision not to remove himself from the case "tells thousands of federal and state judges that it can be OK to vacation with friends who have cases before them and to accept the generosity of those friends while their cases are pending."

In April 2004 Scalia's actions outside Supreme Court chambers once again came under scrutiny. While giving a speech at a Mississippi high school, the justice apparently directed U.S. marshals charged with protecting him to confiscate and erase recordings of his speech made by a teen reporter at the school. "I don't think any public official — and I don't care whether you are a Supreme Court justice or the president of the United States — has a right to speak in public and then say, 'You can't record what I have said,'" said Burt Neuborne, a law professor at New York University. "This doesn't live up to the ideals of the First Amendment. He should know he can't use a U.S. marshal as a private police force to enforce his will."

A Pillar of Modern Conservatism

Despite Scalia's recent struggles in the public spotlight, he remains highly regarded by both legal scholars and America's conservative political community. There has even been speculation that if a Republican is in the Oval Office when Chief Justice Rehnquist decides to retire, Scalia might be nominated to be the new head of the court. Most analysts agree, however, that Scalia would have to endure a bruising confirmation hearing to get the seat, given his long record of opposition to abortion rights, affirmative action, gay rights, church-state separation, and other measures supported by liberal and/or moderate Americans.

Today, Scalia's stature within the Supreme Court seems somewhat unclear. In 2003, for example, the *Los Angeles Times* declared that "although Scalia's views resonate with a large segment of the public, his influence within the court appears to be minimal. Without question, he is smart, quick, witty, and devoted to the law. He is considered the court's most gifted writer, and he often dominates the oral arguments. Yet he rarely writes an important opinion for the court. . . . He is known for his sharply worded dissents — but little else."

"Although Scalia's views resonate with a large segment of the public, his influence within the court appears to be minimal. Without question, he is smart, quick, witty, and devoted to the law. He is considered the court's most gifted writer, and he often dominates the oral arguments. Yet he rarely writes an important opinion for the court. . . . He is known for his sharply worded dissents — but little else."
— Los Angeles Times

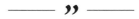

But other analysts see Scalia as a dominant personality, armed with an intellect and reservoir of energy that outshines every other member of the court. And they believe that he will go down as one of the most important Supreme Court justices in U.S. history. "At the most basic level, Justice Scalia is simply a rascal — a brilliant, hilarious rascal who keeps the rest of

A 1986 photo of Justice Scalia with his wife, Maureen, and their nine children.

the court on its feet, but a rascal, nonetheless," stated the *American Spectator.* "So we all need to just sit back and enjoy it. . . . No, collegiality is not Justice Scalia's strong suit, and that fact alone may deny his fans the pleasure of one day seeing a Scalia court. But, honestly, isn't it his Supreme Court already?"

MARRIAGE AND FAMILY

Scalia married Maureen McCarthy on September 10, 1960. Together they raised a family of five boys — Eugene, John, Paul, Matthew, and Christopher — and four girls — Ann, Catherine, Mary Clare, and Margaret Jane. The Scalias make their home in Virginia, near Washington, D.C.

HOBBIES AND OTHER INTERESTS

Scalia enjoys a wide variety of sports, including tennis and squash. He is also an outdoorsman who likes to hunt all sorts of game animals, from deer to pheasant. Other interests include poker and the piano. Finally, Scalia and his wife have traveled widely, journeying to various corners of Europe and Asia.

SELECTED WRITINGS

A Matter of Interpretation: Federal Courts and the Law, 1997

FURTHER READING

Books

Brisbin, Richard A. *Justice Antonin Scalia and the Conservative Revival,* 1997
Hall, Timothy L. *Supreme Court Justices: A Biographical Dictionary,* 2001
Jost, Kenneth, ed. *The Supreme Court, A to Z,* 1998
Lewis, Thomas T., and Richard L. Wilson, eds. *Encyclopedia of the U.S. Supreme Court,* 2001
Maltz, Earl M. *Rehnquist Justice: Understanding the Court Dynamic,* 2003
O'Brien, David M., ed. *Judges on Judging: Views from the Bench,* 1997
Witt, Elder, ed. *Congressional Quarterly's Guide to the U.S. Supreme Court,* 1990
Witt, Elder, ed. *The Supreme Court A to Z: A Ready Reference Encyclopedia,* 1993

Periodicals

ABA Journal, Jan. 1997, Book section, p.86
American Journalism Review, June/July 2004, p.70
American Spectator, Aug./Sep. 2003, p.20
Amicus Journal, Summer 1999, p.34
Commonweal, Mar. 28, 2003, p.11
Current Biography Yearbook, 1986
Dallas Morning News, July 21, 1996, p.J5
GQ, May 2001, p.190
Los Angeles Times, July 9, 1990, p.A1; June 29, 2003, p.A1; Mar. 8, 2004, p.A1; Apr. 9, 2004, p.A18; Apr. 25, 2004, p.A26
Nation, Oct. 9, 2000, p.32; Apr. 19, 2004, p.21
National Review, Dec. 9, 1996, p.34
New Republic, Jan. 18, 1993, p.20; Apr. 5, 2004, p.14
New York Times, June 19, 1986, p.D27; Mar. 15, 1995, p.A22; May 2, 2004, p.A1
Newsweek, Nov. 6, 2000, p.92; July 14, 2003, p.68
Time, June 30, 1986, p.24; July 8, 1996, p.48
USA Today, July 1, 1996, p.A3
Wall Street Journal, Mar. 19, 2004, p.B1
Washington Post, Oct. 17, 2003, p.A27
Washingtonian, Oct. 1998, p.16

Online Articles

http://www.success.org
   (American Success Institute, "Couragously Defend Our Liberty," by Antonin Scalia, undated)

http://www.time.com
   (*Time.com*, "Antonin Scalia, Civil Libertarian," June 14, 2001)

Online Databases

Biography Resource Center Online, 2004, articles from *Contemporary Authors Online,* 2002, and *Encyclopedia of World Biography,* 2004

ADDRESS

Justice Antonin Scalia
U.S. Supreme Court
Supreme Court Building
1 First Street NE
Washington, DC 20543-0002

WORLD WIDE WEB SITES

http://www.supremecourtus.gov
http://www.uscourts.gov
http://www.supremecourthistory.org
http://www.oyez.org

Ben Wallace 1974-

American Professional Basketball Player with
the Detroit Pistons
Two-Time NBA Defensive Player of the Year

BIRTH

Ben Wallace was born in the small, rural community of White
Hall, Alabama, on September 10, 1974. He was the youngest
boy in a family of 11 kids (eight boys and three girls) raised by
their mother, Sadie Wallace, who worked on area farms to
support her children. Ben's birth father, Samuel Doss, was not
a presence during his childhood. The man Wallace regards as
his true father was Freddie Payne, a truck driver.

YOUTH

Wallace was raised in a modest house on the outskirts of Benton, Alabama, a small town about 15 miles outside of Selma. He and his siblings grew up without much in the way of material things—the family did not have a car for years, for example, and their house was the last one in the area to be wired for electricity. According to Wallace, though, his mother managed to raise all her children in a loving and secure environment. "I didn't know people went out every other weekend and bought clothes," he recalled. "It was like I was blind to the real struggle. I just remember being happy."

> "I wasn't really taking the camp seriously, and [Oakley] wanted to show me how serious basketball really was," explained Wallace. "So he beat on me a little bit, and I beat on him a little bit, but I think he was most surprised that I didn't back down. When he hit me underneath the boards, I just kept coming."

Wallace also has warm memories of his father, Freddie Payne. "My father and I were very close," he said. "He never put any pressure on me—he just told me to work hard, to respect myself and respect others."

As a youngster, Wallace spent most of his free time playing basketball and other sports with his older brothers. It was during these rough-and-tumble games that he began to develop the grit and toughness that would be a hallmark of his NBA career. "As the little brother, I knew they weren't going to pass to me," he said. "If I wanted to see the ball, I'd have to get a steal, a rebound, or save the ball from going out of bounds."

By his teen years, Wallace was known around the neighborhood as a formidable opponent on the basketball court. He was bigger and stronger than all of the kids his own age, and he never tired of playing. "He blocked every shot I ever took," recalled one older neighborhood kid who joined Wallace for after-school basketball games. "He'd get out of school, do his homework, and we'd all go play basketball. We'd play almost every day."

Wallace and his siblings also spent a lot of time working on area farms, picking vegetables and bailing hay. Eager to earn a little extra money for himself, he even established a little makeshift barber shop on the front porch of his home during the warm Alabama summers. Watching the street from his seat on the porch, Wallace would flag down passing neighbors and offer them $3 haircuts.

In 1991 Wallace used the money he earned from farm work and cutting hair to secure a spot in a 1991 basketball camp taught by NBA star Charles Oakley. This camp proved to be a pivotal event in Wallace's life. One day at camp, Oakley—who was known as one of the NBA's toughest and most intimidating players—challenged Wallace to a little game of one-on-one in front of the rest of the campers. "I wasn't really taking the camp seriously, and [Oakley] wanted to show me how serious basketball really was," explained Wallace. "So he beat on me a little bit, and I beat on him a little bit, but I think he was most surprised that I didn't back down. When he hit me underneath the boards, I just kept coming."

Charles Oakley was an important influence on Wallace during his early years.

Impressed by Wallace's athleticism and competitive spirit, Oakley spent extra time with the young player for the rest of the camp. By the time Wallace returned home, Oakley had become a sort of mentor to him. In fact, the NBA star remained an important influence in his life for the next several years.

EDUCATION

Wallace attended Central High School in nearby Haynesville, Alabama. He was an all-state performer not only in basketball, but also in football and baseball. "He was a man among boys," recalled a local man who worked as a referee during Wallace's high school years.

As graduation approached, Wallace accepted an athletic scholarship to play football at Auburn, a nationally recognized football powerhouse in the Southeastern Conference. But when his coaches told him that he would not be allowed to play basketball at Auburn, Wallace balked. He decided that if he couldn't play hoops, he wanted to go elsewhere.

Wallace initially set his sights on Virginia Union University (VUU) in Richmond, Virginia, in part because the head basketball coach was a personal friend of Oakley's. When he failed to gain admittance to VUU, Oakley helped him enroll at Cuyahoga Community College in Cleveland in the fall of 1992.

Looking back on his first months in Cleveland, where winter was much more harsh than in Alabama, Wallace said that he might not have stayed were it not for Oakley. "[Attending school in Cleveland] was definitely a shock to me," he said. "I wanted to go home. But Charles went out of his way to be there for me. Whenever I needed to talk on the phone, he was there. I went to his mom's house in Cleveland for home-cooked meals. He gave me a job in his car wash. He committed to me, and he stuck to his word."

As Wallace became more comfortable, his basketball talents blossomed. During his second year at Cuyahoga, he emerged as a dominating floor presence; averaging 24 points, 17 rebounds, and 7 blocked shots per game. At the conclusion of the school year, he returned home to Alabama. He then made a special effort to contact his birth father, who had been completely absent from his life up to that point. "I guess because I was becoming a man myself I was thinking about what I'd be like as a father," Wallace explained. "And I wanted to know his side of the story."

During their meeting, Wallace's birth father—who had fathered 20 children over the years—said that he never visited because he was poor and could not provide financial support to his children. Wallace did not have much patience with this excuse, however. "Nobody asked him for money," he pointed out. "We just wanted a father to be there." Wallace also resented it when his birth father referred to him as "son." "I got a little ticked off," he acknowledged. "I told him, 'My name is Ben. You don't have the right to call me 'Son.'""

In 1994 Wallace's improved grades enabled him to transfer to Virginia Union, a Division II school, which he attended for two years. In the classroom, his emphasis was on criminal justice studies. On the hardcourt, meanwhile, he worked hard to develop his talents so that he could pursue an NBA career.

CAREER HIGHLIGHTS

College — Virginia Union Panthers

After settling in at VUU, Wallace solidified his standing as one of the best big men in the country. He enjoyed a solid junior year, and as a senior he earned Division II All-American honors by averaging 12.5 points and 10.5

Wallace was a strong addition to the team at Virginia Union.

rebounds a game. His presence in the middle helped the Panthers sail to a 28-3 record and a Final Four appearance in the season-ending Division II playoff tournament.

Despite his strong performance, though, Wallace was not selected in the 1996 NBA draft. Pro scouts loved his intensity and his knack for snaring rebounds and blocking shots. But most of them felt that his offensive skills were not polished enough for the NBA. They noted that he did not possess

147

a reliable jump shot, and they agreed that his offensive skills in the low post (the area around the free throw lane near the basket) were mediocre at best.

Wallace was extremely disappointed that he was not drafted, but he refused to give up on his dream of a career in the NBA. When the Boston Celtics invited him to training camp to compete for a spot on the team's roster, he quickly accepted. Upon arrival, though, he discovered that the Celtics wanted to convert him to small forward or even shooting guard. Wallace reluctantly agreed to give it a try, though he secretly thought the decision was foolish. "All my life I played center or forward," he explained. "To come to this league, I knew I might have to change something about my game. But I didn't think I'd have to step off the block [the low post] and start shooting threes. That was drastic. I was a little disappointed by that. But I never swayed from my game. I just figured that hopefully they would see me for what type of player I really was. Even when I did play the two [shooting guard] for Boston in a summer league, I still led the team in rebounds and blocks."

> ―――― " ――――
>
> *"All my life I played center or forward," Wallace explained. "To come to this league, I knew I might have to change something about my game. But I didn't think I'd have to step off the block [the low post] and start shooting threes. That was drastic. I was a little disappointed by that. But I never swayed from my game. I just figured that hopefully they would see me for what type of player I really was."*
>
> ―――― " ――――

Boston's management finally decided that Wallace was not cut out to play guard or small forward. But instead of giving him a try at power forward or center, the team released him. Wallace then played in Italy for a few weeks before being contacted by the NBA's Washington Wizards, who needed to shore up their bench. He quickly returned to the United States, where he earned a spot on the Wizards' roster.

Bouncing Around the NBA

Wallace played his first three NBA seasons with the Wizards. He spent most of his time on the bench, though, despite the Wizards' mediocre performance. His coaches valued Wallace's defensive tenacity and his hard work on the backboards, but his shooting skills — especially at the free throw line—remained poor. As a result, he never cracked the starting line-up, and he averaged only 3.5 points and 5.2 rebounds per game during his time with Washington.

In 1999 Wallace and three other members of the Wizards were traded to the Orlando Magic for Ike Austin. The trade worked out well for Wallace, who saw a lot more floor time with Orlando. In fact, he started 81 games for the Magic at center, averaging 8 rebounds and 1.6 blocked shots a game.

As the 1999 season progressed, Wallace caught the eye of Joe Dumars, a former NBA All-Star with the Detroit Pistons who had become president and general manager of the team after retiring. Dumars recognized that Wallace, despite his heavily muscled physique and large Afro, was actually a little

Wallace bounced around the NBA a bit, playing for the Washington Wizards and the Orlando Magic before landing with the Pistons.

smaller than many other NBA centers. He also saw that the former VUU star's offensive game needed a lot of work. But Dumars felt that "[Wallace] was a physical presence with Orlando, and I thought he'd be a nice pickup for our team."

Landing with the Detroit Pistons

On August 3, 2000, Dumars engineered a trade with Orlando that brought Wallace and a couple other players to Detroit in exchange for Grant Hill. Projected as the Pistons' starting center for the upcoming 2000-01 season, Wallace signed a 6-year, $30 million contract and began working out with the team.

Some NBA analysts questioned the size of the contract that Detroit gave Wallace, citing his limited offensive game. But once the season began, it became clear that a new force had been unleashed in the league. Wallace immediately emerged as the Pistons' defensive anchor, swatting away shots and grabbing rebounds with reckless abandon. By season's end,

Wallace was ranked second in the league in rebounds per game (13.2) and tenth in blocked shots per game (2.33).

The following season, Wallace and the rapidly improving Pistons made even more noise. During the 2001-02 campaign, Wallace averaged more rebounds (13 per game) and blocked more shots (3.48 per game) than anyone else in the NBA. He thus became only the fourth player (after NBA legends Kareem Abdul-Jabbar, Bill Walton, and Hakeem Olajuwon) to accomplish this feat—and the first sub-seven-footer to do so in league history. Wallace's 278 blocked shots also set a new franchise single-season record, obliterating the old mark of 247 held by Hall-of-Famer Bob Lanier. Most important of all, Wallace's rebounding, defense, and occasional scoring (7.6 points per game) helped lift Detroit to a 50-32 record and the Eastern Conference's Central Division title.

> "*We've never seen this kind of dominance from a player this size at the defensive end,*" *said Detroit head coach Rick Carlisle.* "*He does so many things you can't quantify that impact the game. There are no statistics for changing shots, for setting screens, for helping defense, for stepping out on the point guard and then recovering to block his own man's shots.*"

The Pistons were eventually eliminated in the conference playoffs by the Celtics. Despite their brief playoff run, though, the Pistons were clearly a team on the rise. And no one was more responsible for that rise than Wallace. In fact, at season's end he was named the NBA Defensive Player of the Year and honored as a member of the NBA All-Defensive First Team.

As the 2002-03 season approached, coaches, players, and journalists around the NBA were still marveling at Wallace's break-out season. Many of them commented that it was rare to see a player have such a major effect on the outcome of games without scoring. Detroit Head Coach Rick Carlisle admitted that it was unusual. "We've never seen this kind of dominance from a player this size at the defensive end," he said. "He does so many things you can't quantify that impact the game. There are no statistics for changing shots, for setting screens, for helping defense, for stepping out on the point guard and then recovering to block his own man's shots."

Wallace, meanwhile, credited his success to hustle and hard work. "I feel like I'm going to get every rebound," he stated. "If I don't get the ball, I feel like I'm going to get my hand on it. If I can't get my hand on it, I'm going to be as close as I possibly can get to it. I'm definitely going to attack the boards when the shot goes up."

NBA All-Star

During the 2002-03 campaign, Wallace proved that his success was not a fluke. Urged on by Pistons fans who loved his wild Afro and furious playing style, he played so well that he became the first undrafted player ever to be elected to the NBA All-Star Game.

Wallace was delighted by the honor. "We have so many great scorers that some people have to do other things, and that's what I've tried to do," he said. "To come out and play the way I play, not scoring a lot of points, and people still recognize me as one of the best in the league, is an honor."

Unfortunately, Wallace's joy turned to sorrow when his mother died only a few days before the game. "She was the person I always knew I could turn to, the one person who would ask no questions — it'd just be like, 'It's all right, it's all right,'" he said. "If I felt, at times, that I couldn't stick it out, she'd be like, 'Come home, just come home, you can always come home.'" When Wallace went home to Alabama for the funeral, he expressed doubts about playing in the All-Star game. But his family convinced him to play, pointing out that his mother would have wanted him to participate.

After the mid-season All-Star game, Wallace continued to perform at his usual level of excellence. He finished the season among the league leaders in rebounds, averaging 15.4 a game. He also chipped in with 6.9 points and 3.15 blocks per game. These numbers, combined with his relentless defensive pressure, enabled him to clinch a second straight Defensive Player of the Year award.

Wallace's exploits also enabled Detroit to move deeper into the playoffs. After winning their second straight Central Division title with a 50-32 record, the Pistons rolled over Orlando and Philadelphia to advance to the Eastern Conference championship. They came up short against the New Jersey Nets, however, losing in four straight. Wallace finished the playoffs with averages of 8.9 points, 16.3 rebounds, and 3.06 blocks per game.

Beloved in the Motor City

The Pistons entered the 2003-04 season with a new head coach, Larry Brown, and a cast of veterans who were determined to reach the NBA finals. These veterans included fearless point guard Chauncey Billups and

Rebounding has been a key element of Wallace's game.

sharpshooter Richard "Rip" Hamilton, and they were backed by promising young players like all-purpose forward Tayshaun Prince. But the clear fan favorite in the Motor City remained Wallace. For each home game, dozens of fans cheered their team on wearing big Afro wigs to honor the team's hardworking center. "They love [the Afro]," said Wallace. "In fact, they get disappointed and upset when I wear it in corn rows. They're like, 'Hey Ben, when you gonna let the 'fro out? I thought you were going to wear the 'fro!'" His teammates appreciated Wallace's energy as well. "Ben puts life into the building, and he puts life into us," said Billups.

Dumars, meanwhile, expressed amazement at Wallace's transformation into one of Detroit's most beloved athletes. "I had no idea he would become the 'Fro and the two-time defensive player of the year and a sports icon in Detroit—not in my wildest dreams," he said. "He's probably the most popular athlete in Detroit, and he scores seven points a game. I've never seen a player attract so much love." For his part, Wallace offered a simple explanation for his popularity: "My game is what Detroit is all about, hard work."

Detroit started the 2003-04 season with a bang, roaring into the upper ranks of the NBA standings. At mid-season, the Pistons added another weapon when they traded for forward Rasheed Wallace. "When you look back on the team we started with [in my first year], it's a big change," said Ben Wallace. "We've come a long way. It's a totally different team from when I got here. I'm the last one standing. Over the years, we've been able to make a couple changes here and there every year [that have] made the difference."

Driving to a Championship

The Pistons finished the 2003-04 regular season with a 54-28 record, the second-best record in the conference. For the season, Wallace averaged 12.4 rebounds, 3.04 blocks, and 9.5 points per game. His performance gave him the distinction of becoming the first player in NBA history to register 1,000 rebounds, 100 steals, and 100 blocks in the same season. Wallace also made both the All-Star team and the NBA All-Defensive Team for the second straight year.

After knocking off the Milwaukee Bucks in the first round of the playoffs, the Pistons eliminated the New Jersey Nets in a tough seven-game series. In the conference finals they faced the Indiana Pacers, a talented squad led by former Pistons coach Rick Carlisle. The series was a bruising one dominated by defense. In the end, though, the Pistons used the staunch defense of Wallace and Prince and clutch shooting from Hamilton to send the Pacers home in six games.

"I had no idea he would become the 'Fro and the two-time defensive player of the year and a sports icon in Detroit — not in my wildest dreams," Dumars said. "He's probably the most popular athlete in Detroit, and he scores seven points a game. I've never seen a player attract so much love."

The victory over Indiana gave the Pistons their first trip to the NBA finals since 1991, when Dumars and his teammates won their second straight championship. Wallace was thrilled at the opportunity to play in the finals. "It's tough to put this into words," he said. "It's a great feeling to be able to compete for something you've always dreamed of."

As the team prepared for the NBA finals, it found that virtually no one believed that they would emerge victorious. The Pistons' opponent was the Los Angeles Lakers, led by superstars Shaquille O'Neal and Kobe Bryant. Many experts, in fact, predicted that the Lakers would easily sweep the Pistons.

When the series started, however, the Pistons sprung one of the biggest surprises in NBA finals history. Using a deadly combination of stifling defense and team-oriented offense, Detroit crushed the heavily favored

Stifling defense and team-oriented offense — like this rebound Wallace grabbed from the Lakers — were key to the Pistons 2004 championship.

Lakers in five games. The Pistons set the tone for the series in Game One, using smothering defense to claim an 87-75 victory on the Lakers' home court. Los Angeles managed to even the series at 1-1 in Game Two, claiming a 99-91 overtime win. But this contest actually increased the Pistons' confidence, for Wallace and his teammates felt that they had been the better team in both games.

The series then moved to Detroit. In Game Three the Pistons rolled to a decisive 88-68 victory, led by Hamilton's 31 points and a defensive effort that held Bryant and O'Neal to a combined 25 points. In Game Four, the teams were tied going into the fourth quarter. But the Pistons ripped the nets for 32 points in the final stanza to claim an 88-80 victory and a 3-1 series lead.

As Game Five approached, the Lakers talked about their determination to turn the series around. But when the game started, Detroit took command. The Pistons led by as many as 28 points on their way to an easy 100-87 victory. "Nobody gave us a chance against these guys, but we knew all along that we belonged," said Wallace, who exploded for 18 points, 22 rebounds, and three steals in the clinching Game Five. "It's a great feeling. There were a bunch of guys on this team who felt they had something to prove. We added a lot of guys over the last couple of years to get to this point. And we took care of business." It was a gratifying win for the team, and the whole city responded with an outpouring of love and affection.

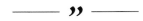

"Nobody gave us a chance against these guys [the LA Lakers], but we knew all along that we belonged," said Wallace, who exploded for 18 points, 22 rebounds, and three steals in the clinching Game Five of the NAB finals. "It's a great feeling. There were a bunch of guys on this team who felt they had something to prove. We added a lot of guys over the last couple of years to get to this point. And we took care of business."

Looking to Repeat

In recognition of their terrific performances in the playoffs, both Wallace and Hamilton were invited to play on the Team USA basketball team in the 2004 Summer Olympics in Athens, Greece. Both men declined, however, citing fatigue from their long run to the NBA title and terrorist-related concerns about the safety of their families.

In August 2004 Wallace underwent successful emergency surgery for acute appendicitis. He was held out of the beginning of training camp so that he could make a full recovery from the surgery.

As the 2004-05 season approached, Wallace expressed great confidence about Detroit's chances of successfully defending their NBA crown. "Winning the championship is something everybody wanted to do," he declared. "With the type of team we have, everyone is geared up to make this run again."

But some of that confidence was squandered early in the season, when a fight broke out at a Pistons game against the Indiana Pacers. A fierce rivalry exists between the teams, since the Pistons had beaten the Pacers in the semi-finals the previous season. Late in the game, with the Pistons losing by 15 points, Ron Artest fouled Wallace, who responded by angrily shoving him back. A few minutes later, Artest was laying down on the scorers' table when a fan in the stands threw a plastic cup on his face. That started a brawl in which Artest and several other Pacers jumped into the stands and fought with fans. A dispiriting range of ugly behavior followed, including players and fans fighting on the court, as well as fans pelting the players with beer, popcorn, and other trash. Someone even threw a metal folding chair at the players' heads.

> "
>
> *"I like coming back home,"*
> *Wallace said. "Do it every*
> *Fourth of July. Everybody's*
> *cooking, and I'm just being*
> *Ben, like the little kid*
> *I was running around the*
> *neighborhood."*
>
> "

After the incident, blame was quickly assigned to all parties. The Indiana players were condemned for losing their cool and going into the stands to attack the fans, and the Detroit fans were condemned for their aggressive behavior toward the Indiana players. Heavy penalties were levied against several players on each team, with the most severe being a full-season suspension for Ron Artest. Wallace was suspended for six games for his role in the altercation. After the goodwill and happiness the Pistons and the Detroit fans had enjoyed the previous season, it was a disappointing way to begin the season.

MARRIAGE AND FAMILY

Wallace and his wife Chanda have three children. They live in Virginia during the off-season, but Wallace regularly returns to Alabama to see family and friends. "I like coming back home," he said. "Do it every Fourth of July.

Everybody's cooking, and I'm just being Ben, like the little kid I was running around the neighborhood."

HOBBIES AND OTHER INTERESTS

Friends, teammates, and family all say that at heart, Wallace is a "big kid." For example, he enjoys collecting remote-control cars and going motorbiking with kids around his neighborhood. Wallace also enjoys hunting, fishing, swimming, and other outdoor activities.

HONORS AND AWARDS

Division II All-American: 1996
NBA Defensive Player of the Year: 2001-02, 2002-03
NBA All-Defensive Team: 2001-02, 2003-04
All-NBA Second Team: 2002-03, 2003-04
NBA All-Star: 2003, 2004

FURTHER READING

Books

Detroit Free Press. *Men at Work: The 2004 NBA Champions,* 2004
Detroit News. *Detroit Pistons: Champions at Work,* 2004
Who's Who among African-Americans, 2004

Periodicals

Basketball Digest, Summer 2002, p.42; Mar.-Apr. 2004, p.20; July-Aug. 2004,
    p.40
Birmingham (Ala.) News, July 4, 2004, Sports
Current Biography Yearbook, 2004
Detroit Free Press, Apr. 19, 2004
Detroit News, Apr. 4, 2003, p.H4; Dec. 1, 2003, p.D4; June 16, 2004, p.A1
ESPN Magazine, Mar. 3, 2003, p.40
GQ, Dec. 2003, p.170
Los Angeles Times, June 16, 2004, p.S7
Montgomery (Ala.) Advertiser, July 4, 2004, p.A1
New York Times, May 11, 2002, p.D1; July 4, 2004, p.SP1
Sports Illustrated, Mar. 9, 1998, p.103; Oct. 29, 2001, p.150; Feb. 10, 2003,
    p.42; June 21, 2004, p.48; June 30, 2004 (special issue)
Sports Illustrated for Kids, Nov. 2004, p.24
USA Today, June 4, 2004, p.C21

Washington Post, May 1, 1999, p.D6; Apr. 24, 2002, p.D1; June 16, 2004, p.A1; June 16, 2004, p.D1

Online Articles

http://www.hoopshype.com
  (*Hoopshype.com,* "Ben Wallace: "Once You Win, Everybody Gets Recognized," Apr. 21, 2002)
http://www.insidehoops.com/wallace-interview-060604.shtml
  (*Insidehoops.com,* "Ben Wallace Interview," June 6, 2004)
http://www.nba.com/news/wallace_030423.html
  (*NBA.com,* "Wallace Named Defensive Player of the Year," Apr. 23, 2004)

Online Databases

Biography Resource Center Online, 2004, article from *Who's Who among African Americans,* 2004

ADDRESS

Ben Wallace
Detroit Pistons
Palace of Auburn Hills
Four Championship Drive
Auburn Hills, MI 48326

WORLD WIDE WEB SITES

http://www.nba.com/players
http://sports.espn.go.com/nba/index
http://sportsillustrated.cnn.com/basketball/nba/players

Photo and Illustration Credits

Jack Black/Photos: Kevin Winter/Getty Images (p. 9); Melissa Mosely/copyright © Touchstone Pictures. All Rights Reserved (p. 14); Joe Ledrer/copyright © 2001 Columbia Pictures Industries, Inc. (*Silverman*/p. 16); Glenn Watson/copyright © 2001 Twentieth Century Fox (*Hal*/p. 16); Gemma LaMana/TM & copyright © 2001 by Paramount Pictures (*County*/p. 16); TM & copyright © 2003 by Paramount Pictures (cover photo, p. 19); Brian Hamill/TM & copyright © 2004 Dreamworks LLC and Columbia Pictures Industries, Inc. (p. 20). CD cover: Epic/copyright © 2001 Sony Music Entertainment Inc./(P) 2001 Sony Music Entertainment Inc.

Eve/Photos: Monty Brinton/copyright © 2003 UPN (p. 24); Tracy Bennett/ copyright © 2002 Metro-Goldwyn-Mayer Pictures, Inc.(p. 31); Ron Jaffe/copyright © 2004 Warner Bros. All Rights Reserved (p. 33); Adger Cowans (p. 35). CD covers: LET THERE BE EVE copyright © 1999 Ruff Ryders/Interscope Records; SCORPION copyright © 2001 Ruff Ryders/ Interscope Records. Cover photo: Monty Brinton/copyright © 2003 UPN.

Jennie Finch/Photos: Robert Laberge/Getty Images (p. 39); AP/Wide World Photos (p. 42); Chris McGrath/Getty Images (p. 44); Getty Images (p. 47).

Wally Funk/Photos: Matthew Mahon (p. 49); Wally Funk (pp. 52, 55, 57); NASA (p. 59).

T.D. Jakes/Photos: courtesy The Potter's House (pp. 63, 74); AP/Wide World Photos (rpp. 68, 71). Cover: WOMAN, THOU ART LOOSED! (Berkley Books) copyright © 2004 by T.D. Jakes. CD cover: (P) & © copyright 2001 EMI Gospel. Cover photo: AP/Wide World Photos.

Toby Keith/Photos: AP/Wide World Photos (p. 79); Reuters (p. 84); Reuters/Joe Skipper/ Landov (p. 89). CD covers: TOBY KEITH (P) & © copyright 1993 Mercury Records; UNLEASHED (P) & © copyright 2002 SKG Music Nashville LLC; SHOCK'N Y'ALL (P) & © copyright 2003 SKG Music Nashville LLC.

Karen Michell-Raptakis/Photos: Karen Mitchell-Raptakis (pp. 94, 102). Card covers: copyright © 2000 by the LDC Design Company, Inc.

Queen Noor/Photos: Mehdi Fedouach/AFP/Getty Images (p. 107); AP/Wide World Photos (p. 109, 123); copyright © Bettmann/CORBIS (p. 115); AFP/Getty Images (p. 117); copyright © Nader/CORBIS Sygma (p. 119); copyright © Norman Parkinson Limited/Fiona Cowan/CORBIS (p. 126). Cover: LEAP OF FAITH (Miramax Books) copyright © 2003 by Her Majesty Queen Noor. Map: © 2001 Map Resources. Cover photo: Gustavo Cuevas/EPA/Landov.

Antonin Scalia/Photos: AP/Wide World Photos (pp. 128, 130, 138, 140); copyright © Bettmann/CORBIS (p. 133). Cover: A MATTER OF INTERPRETATION copyright © 1997 by Princeton University Press.

Ben Wallace/Photos: Allen Einstein/NBAE/Getty Images (p. 143, 154); Joe Patronite/ Getty Images (p. 145); Virginia Union University (p. 147); Andy Lyons/Getty Images (p. 149); Nathaniel S. Butler/NBAE/Getty Images (p. 152).

Cumulative Names Index

This cumulative index includes the names of all individuals profiled in *Biography Today* since the debut of the series in 1992.

For cumulative general, places of birth, and birthday indexes, please see www.biographytoday.com.

Biography Today

General Series

Biography Today **General Series** includes a unique combination of current biographical profiles that teachers and librarians — and the readers themselves — tell us are most appealing. The **General Series** is available as a 3-issue subscription; hardcover annual cumulation; or subscription plus cumulation.

Within the **General Series**, your readers will find a variety of sketches about:

- Authors
- Musicians
- Political leaders
- Sports figures
- Movie actresses & actors
- Cartoonists
- Scientists
- Astronauts
- TV personalities
- and the movers & shakers in many other fields!

"Biography Today will be useful in elementary and middle school libraries and in public library children's collections where there is a need for biographies of current personalities. High schools serving reluctant readers may also want to consider a subscription."
— *Booklist,* American Library Association

"Highly recommended for the young adult audience. Readers will delight in the accessible, energetic, tell-all style; teachers, librarians, and parents will welcome the clever format, intelligent and informative text. It should prove especially useful in motivating 'reluctant' readers or literate nonreaders."
— *MultiCultural Review*

"Written in a friendly, almost chatty tone, the profiles offer quick, objective information. While coverage of current figures makes *Biography Today* a useful reference tool, an appealing format and wide scope make it a fun resource to browse." — *School Library Journal*

"The best source for current information at a level kids can understand."
— Kelly Bryant, School Librarian, Carlton, OR

"Easy for kids to read. We love it! Don't want to be without it."
— Lynn McWhirter, School Librarian, Rockford, IL

ONE-YEAR SUBSCRIPTION
- 3 softcover issues, 6" x 9"
- Published in January, April, and September
- 1-year subscription, $60
- 150 pages per issue
- 10 profiles per issue
- Contact sources for additional information
- Cumulative Names Index

HARDBOUND ANNUAL CUMULATION
- Sturdy 6" x 9" hardbound volume
- Published in December
- $62 per volume
- 450 pages per volume
- 25-30 profiles — includes all profiles found in softcover issues for that calendar year
- Cumulative General Index

SUBSCRIPTION AND CUMULATION COMBINATION
- $99 for 3 softcover issues plus the hardbound volume

For Cumulative General, Places of Birth, and Birthday Indexes, please see www.biographytoday.com.

Biography Today

Subject Series

Expands and complements the General Series and targets specific subject areas . . .

Our readers asked for it! They wanted more biographies, and the *Biography Today* **Subject Series** is our response to that demand. Now your readers can choose their special areas of interest and go on to read about their favorites in those fields. Priced at just $39 per volume, the following specific volumes are included in the *Biography Today* **Subject Series**:

- **Authors**
- **Business Leaders**
- **Performing Artists**
- **Scientists & Inventors**
- **Sports**

FEATURES AND FORMAT

- Sturdy 6" x 9" hardbound volumes
- Individual volumes, $39 each
- 200 pages per volume
- 10 profiles per volume — targets individuals within a specific subject area
- Contact sources for additional information
- Cumulative General Index

For Cumulative General, Places of Birth, and Birthday Indexes, please see www.biographytoday.com.

NOTE: There is *no duplication of entries* between the **General Series** of *Biography Today* and the **Subject Series**.

AUTHORS

"A useful tool for children's assignment needs." — *School Library Journal*

"The prose is workmanlike: report writers will find enough detail to begin sound investigations, and browsers are likely to find someone of interest." — *School Library Journal*

SCIENTISTS & INVENTORS

"The articles are readable, attractively laid out, and touch on important points that will suit assignment needs. Browsers will note the clear writing and interesting details." — *School Library Journal*

"The book is excellent for demonstrating that scientists are real people with widely diverse backgrounds and personal interests. The biographies are fascinating to read." — *The Science Teacher*

SPORTS

"This series should become a standard resource in libraries that serve intermediate students." — *School Library Journal*